CREATIVE WOODWORKING

JAYNE DROTNING
AND
ROSEMARIE MASOTTO

Photography by Tom Masotto

Contemporary Books, Inc.
Chicago

Library of Congress Cataloging in Publication Data

Drotning, Jayne.
  Creative woodworking.

  Includes index.
  1. Woodwork.   I. Masotto, Rosemarie, joint author.
II. Title
TT194.D76   1979   684'.08   79-50973
ISBN 0-8092-7158-3
ISBN 0-8092-7157-5 pbk.

Every effort has been made to assure the accuracy of the instructions in this book, but no warranty is given nor are results guaranteed. The authors and the publisher have no control over the conditions in which the information is applied and consequently disclaim any responsibility for the results obtained.

The projects in this book were designed by Jayne Drotning, unless otherwise noted. They are presented for the personal use of individual readers and may not be reproduced for sale by commercial enterprises without the express permission of the designer.

Published by Contemporary Books, Inc.
180 North Michigan Avenue, Chicago, Illinois 60601
Manufactured in the United States of America
Library of Congress Catalog Card Number: 79-50973
International Standard Book Number: 0-8092-7158-3 (cloth)
                                    0-8092-7157-5 (paper)

Published simultaneously in Canada by
Beaverbooks
953 Dillingham Road
Pickering, Ontario L1W 1Z7
Canada

Contents

Introduction

Woodworking with power equipment, a fascinating hobby long enjoyed by men, has begun to attract many craft-oriented women as well. Thousands of housewives and career women, no longer challenged by the traditional needlecrafts, have discovered inexpensive light-weight power tools that can be set up on the kitchen counter, or almost anywhere else in the home, and stored as easily. They find them an exciting new outlet for their creative talents and energy and are learning—often to their surprise—that power equipment is neither as awesome nor as difficult to master as they had supposed. Once they have overcome that hangup they are soon delighted to discover the creative potential of beautiful, useful, and inexpensive objects fashioned from wood.

Although this book is of equal value to men, it has a special focus for women who may have avoided power tools because they are unaware of the compact power equipment that is now available. Its message is simple: Operating light-weight scroll saws, table saws, lathes and power carvers is almost as safe as running a vacuum cleaner and less complicated than operating a sewing machine *if* you know what you are doing. You need only to appreciate their versatility and be aware of their limitations, to learn a few simple operating techniques and shortcuts which are described in this book, and to abide by a few basic safety rules.

You don't have to serve a five-year apprenticeship with a master craftsman before you begin to take pride in your work. The pages that follow will guide you quickly through the learning curve so that you can develop proficiency in a matter of hours, not weeks or months. You will learn how to select and use equipment and materials; how to make patterns; and how to carve, paint, and decorate the objects that you create.

Included in this book are designs and patterns for an infinite variety of projects that you can undertake to brighten your home, give as gifts to delight your friends, create as fast-selling money-makers to supplement your income, or raise money with at your favorite charity bazaar. You'll be delighted to discover that many of the things you have already made of paper, felt, and yarn can be duplicated, more beautifully and permanently, in wood. Even more exciting are the useful tips it offers on how to develop your "creative eye" so that you can design and produce unique projects that are your very own.

1 What you need to get started

Most of us have known men who had a sudden urge to try their hand at woodworking and began by equipping their basement workshop with hundreds of dollars worth of sophisticated power tools. Too often, these impetuous enthusiasts were so overwhelmed by the complexities of their fancy new machinery that their first project never got off the ground.

Don't let that happen to you!

As you develop proficiency and seek new challenges you will probably want to add more versatile and efficient equipment, but don't launch your venture into woodcrafts by buying out the hardware store. We don't recommend you try, but it is literally possible to make every project in this book with hand tools, most of which are probably in your house right now. You'll be able to work more efficiently and effectively, however, if you equip yourself with some of the power tools that are now available to home hobbyists.

Figures 1–3 illustrate some of the hand tools that will be useful in completing your projects. Begin with a scissors, hammer, screwdriver, pliers, ruler, yardstick, square and T-square, Elmer's Carpenter's glue, a supply of fine and medium grade garnet or aluminum oxide paper, and lots of sharp pencils. As you proceed, you'll save time and energy if you add a flat and round rasp, a hand-sanding block, C-clamps, a drill guide, two or three sizes of Disston Abraders, and a power drill.

THE DREMEL MOTO-SHOP

The basic tool of your new craft experience will be a jigsaw or scroll saw designed for home workshop use. There are several models on the market. The one used to create the designs in this book is the Dremel Moto-Shop (Figure 4), which costs about seventy dollars. Cheaper models are available but they lack the versatility of the Moto-Shop. It is almost literally a small home workshop in one compact

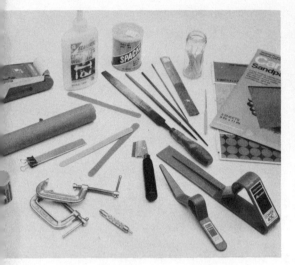

Figs. 1–3. Basic hand tools

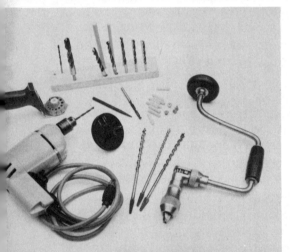

unit, so light that it can be set up on a kitchen counter and tucked away in a cupboard when not in use. The unique feature of the Moto-Shop is a power take-off that turns a disk, supplied with the saw, for sanding, buffing, polishing, and deburring. The deluxe model also includes a flexible shaft with attachments that can be used for drilling, routing, carving, engraving, grinding, sharpening, and other purposes. This equipment can also be bought separately as an attachment for the basic Moto-Shop.

The Moto-Shop will cut softwood up to $1\frac{3}{4}$-inches thick, and hardwood up to $\frac{1}{2}$-inch thick. It has a throat capacity of fifteen inches. This is the distance between the blade and the upright member that supports the upper arm of the saw, which limits the length of the cut you can make when work is fed directly into the saw. The saw will

Fig. 4. Dremel Moto-Shop

also cut plastic, Masonite, copper to eighteen gauge, and aluminum to ¼-inch thick.

Woodworking hobbyists owe a large debt to Albert J. Dremel, who invented the Moto-Shop. An Austrian immigrant, he came to America penniless in 1906 and became one of the classic self-made men of the Industrial Revolution. He learned mechanical drawing by taking a correspondence course and went on to become a designer for several industrial giants. During his career he invented the first safe electric wringer attachment for a washing machine, the first walk-behind power lawnmower, and dozens of other useful devices. He will be remembered, however, as the father of hobby workshops because he invented seven small portable power tools for home workshop use.

THE DREMEL MOTO-TOOL

You can increase the range of creative woodworking projects you undertake by equipping yourself with another of Mr. Dremel's inventions, a power woodcarver called the Moto-Tool (Figure 5). The Moto-Tool is the answer to a woodcarver's prayers for it cuts hardwood easily and will carve in minutes what would take hours with a knife. There are several models available and many accessories, including a drill press stand, a Moto-Tool holder, a D-Vise, and a router attachment.

You may some day wish to acquire two other members of the Dremel woodworking arsenal. The Moto-Lathe (Figure 6) is a valuable tool for those interested in building miniature furniture and for turning wood to other uses. For light work, the newest Dremel product, a four-inch table saw (Figure 7), is an effective substitute for the heavy and ungainly table and radial arm saws found in most home workshops. At the outset your Moto-Shop will suffice, but as you delve more deeply into woodcrafts you may want to add a table saw to your workshop for greater speed and accuracy in mitering joints and making straight cuts. Like other Dremel products, the table saw weighs only a few pounds, can be set up almost anywhere in minutes, then stored away in a kitchen cupboard.

Remember, don't over-equip yourself at the outset. Begin with the Moto-Shop and—if you plan to carve—the Moto-Tool. Add other equipment as you get more deeply into your new hobby and your need for it becomes apparent. A gentle hint dropped to your spouse, when a particularly attractive piece of your work is being admired, may yield another piece of woodworking equipment next Christmas!

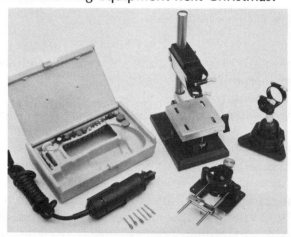

Fig. 5. Dremel Moto-Tool
and accessories

Fig. 6. Dremel Moto-Lathe and accessories   Fig. 7. Dremel 4-inch table saw

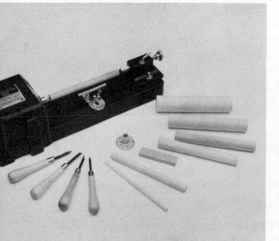

2 A word about safety

Some men and many women share an inherent fear of power tools. If you are among them, it isn't all bad. It will encourage you to approach them with an appropriate degree of caution while you discover for yourself that there is nothing to fear if you treat power equipment with respect.

The Moto-Shop is equipped with a very effective blade guard, which also serves as a hold-down device to keep your work in place. The metal guard on the saw used in this book has recently been redesigned. The new guard, made of plastic, will also keep your fingers away from the blade, but does not have to be lifted manually when you feed work into the saw.

The important thing to remember whenever you flip the switch on your saw, is that even the best of safety devices isn't worth a darn if you detach it from the machine. Some operations require that the guard be removed and, at these times, extra caution is required. Don't ever become impatient, however, and detach the guard to simplify an operation or save a little time.

The major hazards of power tool operation are impatience, carelessness, fatigue, and inattention. Concentrate on what you are doing; don't operate the equipment when you are overtired; and never, never, decide to bypass some safety precaution because you are in a hurry, telling yourself that you can do it "just this once." It only takes "once" to have an unfortunate accident.

Remember, too, that your respect for the saw will diminish as your confidence increases. "Familiarity breeds contempt" applies to machines as well as people. The more skilled you are with the equipment the more careless you are apt to become. Never forget that the saw hasn't changed even though your attitude has; the potential for a cut finger will always remain if you fail to exercise appropriate care.

KEEP AN EYE ON THE KIDS

We have already noted that all of the Dremel power tools can be set up in almost any location that has an electrical outlet nearby. They spare you the need to set aside space for a workshop. The Moto-Shop that cut the objects in this book was set up on an island counter in the author's kitchen. While this flexibility is a real boon, it can also present a hazard if there are children in your house. They may distract you from your work, increasing the chances that *you* may have an accident; they may be tempted to play with your saw and other equipment, increasing the possibility that *they* may have one, too; so, don't work when the kids are underfoot. Always turn the saw off when you are not using it, and always disconnect the power cord when your saw is not in view. Anchor the power cord with the clip so that it cannot accidentally come into contact with the saw blade or sanding disk. Take similar precautions with your hand tools, for in a child's hands some of them can be dangerous, too. Take out only the hand tools that you intend to use; keep an eye on them while you are working; and put them away when you are through. Sharp blades and saws are dangerously attractive to children, and even a hammer can smash the fingers of small children trying to imitate what they have seen you do.

If the power equipment you are using has a three-prong electrical plug it is there for a reason—to keep you from getting an electrical shock while operating the machine. If your wall receptacle doesn't accommodate the plug, buy an adapter and be sure to attach the ground tab to the screw in the wall plate when you plug it in. Don't be tempted to use an ordinary extension cord and let the third prong dangle in the air, for if you do, the electrical shock hazard will still be there.

KEEP WORK AREA CLEAN

Keep the floor in your work area clean and free of scrap lumber and other obstructions. Many an accident has occurred when the person operating the saw stumbled on a block of wood. Never work on a wet surface because it exposes you to the possibility of a serious, even fatal, electrical shock.

If you are attempting an intricate operation that requires removal of the blade guard, devise some alternate means of protecting yourself from an accidental slip that will expose your fingers to the blade.

Don't force your power equipment to work beyond its rated capacity or perform tasks for which it was not designed. Whether you are using the jigsaw, Moto-Tool, or Moto-Lathe, remember not to apply excessive force. The tool, not you, should do the work.

Fig. 8. Using D-Vise to hold work   Fig. 9. Using Moto-Tool holder

Don't wear loose clothing, or work with necklaces or long hair dangling because they might get caught in the machine. It is also wise to wear safety glasses at all times, and a dust mask if you are doing particularly dusty work.

Always disconnect your power equipment before servicing it, changing blades or accessories. Avoid unintentional starting by making sure that the switch is in the "off" position before plugging in the equipment.

Never leave any piece of power equipment running unattended. It may prove too tempting for the children in the house. Don't allow your children to play with the saw or operate it when an adult is not present. Until they are into their teens, most children simply do not have the concentration that enables them to safely operate power woodworking equipment without supervision.

Don't perform sawing operations with the Moto-Shop when the attachments are in place. The sanding disk and flexible shaft reduce the power of the saw and also present a needless hazard to the operator. For example, if you saw while the sanding disk is attached and turning, it is easy to sand the skin off a knuckle because you have forgotten that the disk was there.

Whenever possible, Moto-Tool users should use clamps or the Dremel D-Vise to hold their work in place (Figure 8). It is not only safer, but also more accurate and convenient because the work is held firmly, leaving both hands free to operate the tool. An alternative is to use the Moto-Tool holder or drill press to hold the tool in place while your hands maneuver the work (Figure 9).

It is important to keep your tools sharp and clean in order to obtain the best and safest performance from them. Be sure to remove keys and adjusting wrenches from your Moto-Tool or other power equipment so they don't fly off when you turn the power on.

Follow these guidelines and you will enjoy countless safe, happy hours with your power equipment. Never forget, properly used power tools are not dangerous, but sometimes their operator is!

3 How to use this book

"Practice makes perfect" is a cliché that applies to woodworking as it has to most of the other skills acquired during your lifetime. Disappointment and frustration are the twin adversaries of the beginning woodworker. You are most likely to experience them if you are impatient, neglect to learn basic techniques by practicing them, or attempt the most difficult projects before you have sharpened your skills by mastering the simpler techniques. You'll find that this is not a long, drawn-out process, but it is an essential first step.

Get the "feel" of the jigsaw by practicing on scrap material and then moving on to flat projects that do not require intricate, delicate cuts. This will help you to develop your skill while completing attractive pieces that will give you a real sense of accomplishment almost at once. You'll be happier with a simple project done well than with a difficult one done badly.

When you are comfortable cutting flat projects, move on to boxes. Try a simple square or rectangular box—first with butt joints and then with mitered ones (see "Types of Joints"). Once you have learned to make a simple box, you'll have the skill to make others in any size or shape, to build miniature houses, trays, and other similar designs. Now you're ready to try cylindrical containers and other shapes and construction forms that are patterned later in the book.

Finally, try some of the three-dimensional objects that require you to glue several pieces of wood together, or carve with the Moto-Tool. Remember, your Moto-Shop works best on stock up to one-inch thick. To make an object three-inches thick it is easiest to cut three identical one-inch pieces, glue them together, and then sand the edges until the surface is smooth.

Although this book is primarily devoted to working with wood, we have included a few projects that will stimulate your imagination in using combinations of wood and other materials. Some examples of decoupage decoration are included to provide quick, easy projects to do when you're not in a mood to paint. Other projects involve

8

combinations of wood and macrame, or wood and acrylic plastic, which can be cut on the Moto-Shop and engraved with the Moto-Tool. A few examples of miniature furniture, cut entirely on the scroll saw, are provided to stimulate you to design some of your own.

HOW TO USE PATTERNS

Most of the projects in the book can be completed by following the general instructions that follow. Special techniques are described in the text accompanying some of the patterns. When possible, full-scale patterns are provided, but patterns for larger objects must be enlarged using the transfer-by-squares process. These patterns are shown on grids and can be altered to any dimension by transferring them square-by-square to larger or smaller grids. To transfer a pattern from one grid to another, simply copy the contents of each first-grid square on the corresponding second-grid square. In virtually all cases you will be transferring to a grid of ½-inch by ½-inch squares (exceptions are indicated where necessary). After transferring the pattern free-hand, refine your drawing using a ruler and French curve.

Patterns may be traced onto tracing paper placed over the page, or by placing a sheet of carbon under the page and going over the pattern outline with a stylus. In some cases, when both sides of a part are identical, only half the pattern is shown. To create the full pattern draw a line on tracing paper and line it up with the broken pattern line. Trace the pattern; fold the paper in half and trace the other half. Unfold the paper and you have the complete pattern, ready to use. If the half-pattern is one that must be enlarged make your transfer-by-squares *before* you go through the tracing process just described.

When you have completed your pattern, transfer it to the wood by tracing with graphite paper (Figure 10) or by gluing the pattern to the wood with rubber cement. The latter technique destroys the pattern and should not be used if the project is one you may want to repeat. Be sure the pattern lines are dark so that you can see them clearly when you begin to saw. You can save stock by placing the patterns carefully on the wood, but don't try to cut two pieces from a single dividing pattern line until you become really skilled with the saw. Remember, only the cutting lines should be transferred to the wood. Wait to transfer the painting pattern until after the base coat of gesso has been applied or you won't be able to see the lines. You will find more information on patterns in chapter 7.

SANDING YOUR WORK

Chapter 4 includes instructions on the operation of the Moto-Shop. Study them before you begin to use the saw. When you have completed cutting a project, sand all surfaces and edges until they are smooth. Avoid excessive edge sanding, which may alter dimensions so that the parts of a project no longer fit.

If the object is to be painted, sawing errors and defects in materials should be repaired with plastic wood before sanding. If the project is one that will be stained or finished naturally, it is almost impossible to match these patches so that they don't show. The solution is to select wood for such projects that is totally free of defects and saw it with exceptional care.

The sanding disk attachment which slips easily into the power takeoff on your Moto-Shop can be used to sand large areas and, if you do it carefully, to round and smooth the edges of your work (Figure 11). If you have a good eye you can also bevel edges with the sanding disk (Figure 12).

A flat hand-sander is also useful for sanding and rounding edges. The amount of edge sanding required will vary depending on the type of wood being sawed, the accuracy of the cut, and the coarseness of the blade. If the edge is very rough, a flat, coarse Disston Abrader will smooth it quickly (Figure 13). Finish with medium or fine-grade paper on a flat hand-sander. Interior cuts may be sanded with fine abrasive paper rolled around a round dowel (Figure 14) or a flat stick (Figure 15) of the appropriate size. You can also use a pointed Disston Abrader or various sizes of files and rasps. Holes can be enlarged and lined up with a round rasp.

The sanding drums and disks that accompany the Moto-Tool are particularly effective for many sanding chores, particularly for sanding interior cuts. They chew away wood very rapidly, however, so be sure to use a delicate touch.

A standard "fine" grade abrasive paper is adequate for the final sanding on an object that is to be painted. To achieve perfection always sand with the grain. Carved items that will be finished with varnish, shellac, or clear wood finishes, like Deft, should be finished by sanding with even finer grades, and by giving them a final treatment with extra fine steel wool.

Don't use flint paper; garnet or aluminum oxide paper works better and lasts longer. These abrasive papers are graded by two different methods: Medium will be designated 1/2, 0, 2/0, or 60, 80, 100; fine is 3/0, 4/0, 5/0, or 120, 150, 180; and extra fine ranges from 6/0 to 10/0, or 220, 240, 280, 320, and 400. Experimentation will determine the most suitable grade for the project at hand.

GLUING AND ASSEMBLING

Before assembling your projects check all parts to make sure they fit. The best way to be sure is to actually assemble the project,

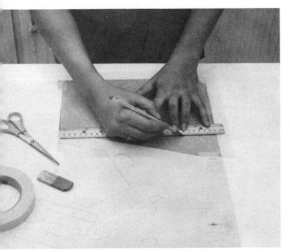

Fig. 10. Tracing pattern on wood

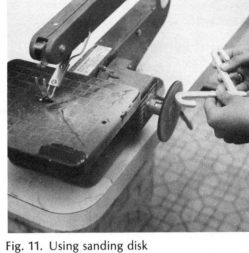

Fig. 11. Using sanding disk

Fig. 12. Beveling with sanding disk

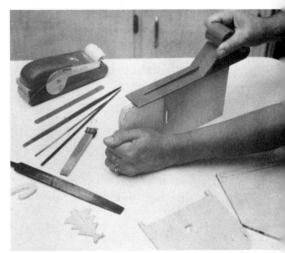

Fig. 13. Using Disston Abrader

Fig. 14. Sanding with paper around dowel

Fig. 15. Sanding with paper around flat stick

Fig. 16. Applying glue

fastening the parts with masking tape. Some woodworkers paint the parts before they are assembled, so that they can work on flat surfaces, but this then requires that joints and nail holes be touched up after assembly. It's a nuisance to paint the interior of an assembled box! When painting individual parts be careful to avoid applying paint to surfaces that must later be glued together, or they may not hold firmly.

Avoid using too much glue. It can actually weaken the bond, and if it is squeezed onto a surface that is to receive a stain or natural finish you may have a problem. Even if you wipe it off immediately it will seal the wood and that spot will not take a stain when you apply it later, unless you sand all the glue off first.

There are several brands of commercial wood glue that will hold your projects firmly together. You may wish to experiment with several to determine which you prefer. The projects in this book were joined with Elmer's Carpenter's glue, which sets quickly and makes a very strong bond. After making sure that the parts being glued are dry and free from dust or dirt, squeeze a bit of glue onto the plastic cover of a margarine cup and apply it to both surfaces with a toothpick or cotton swab (Figure 16).

After the glue has been applied the parts can be held together with clamps, heavy rubber bands, or bound tightly with string. Flat surfaces can be held in place with weights. On light objects, if you use Elmer's Carpenter's glue, these measures are often unnecessary.

Instead, allow the glue to become a bit tacky before joining the parts and simply hold them together for a minute or so.

REINFORCING JOINTS

Joints that will be subjected to stress should be fastened with nails or dowels as well as glue to provide added strength. These fasteners will also help to hold the pieces in position while the glue dries. When nailing into the edges of plywood, you must use fine wire nails or the plywood will split (Figure 17). On larger items, particularly those that must bear weight, you may use screws, countersinking the heads (Figure 18) so that they can be concealed with plastic wood or by inserting dowel.

To fasten two pieces with dowel, hold them firmly in place and drill all the way through one piece and partway into the other. Then insert a dowel that is $\frac{1}{8}$-inch shorter than the hole you have drilled so that you can countersink it and fill the surface depression with plastic wood. To drill a hole to a specific depth, wrap a piece of masking tape around the drill bit to mark the required depth (Figure 19).

It is critical when drilling holes for a dowel to be certain that they line up perfectly and are in an exactly vertical position. If not, the parts will not join accurately. A drill guide (Figure 20) or drill press will help you drill a straight hole for the size dowel needed for the job. The Portalign precision drill guide, recently introduced, is a useful tool for drilling straight holes, drilling holes in dowel, drilling at precise angles, and to a specific depth.

Your work will be more attractive if you install blind dowels so that ends are not exposed and no filling is required. To install a blind dowel, drill a hole to the proper depth in one piece and use a dowel kit to mark the precise location of the dowel hole on the matching piece. These kits can be purchased for various sizes of dowel. A disk with a point in the center is inserted in the first hole you drill and placed carefully against the second piece at precisely the point where the dowel will be inserted (Figure 21). When you press the two pieces of wood together, the point marks the spot where the second hole should be drilled. Drilling into an irregularly shaped piece is difficult. Avoid doing this by drilling holes before pieces are cut out. This will enable you to work with flat surfaces (Figure 22).

Before inserting a dowel it is wise, though not essential, to chamfer the ends so it will insert more readily. This can be done with the sanding disk on your Moto-Shop or Moto-Tool. The circular saw blade on the Moto-Tool can also be used to cut a groove the length of the dowel that will accept excess glue. When assembling the piece,

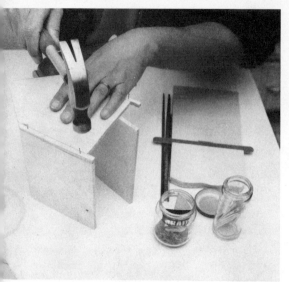

Fig. 17. Nailing joint

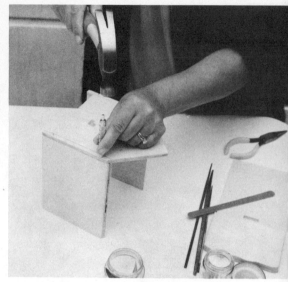

Fig. 18. Setting nail

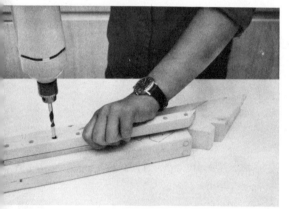

Fig. 19. Using tape to mark depth

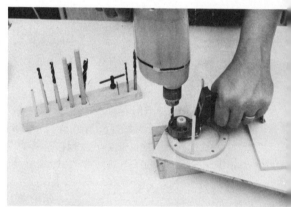

Fig. 20. Using drill guide

Fig. 21. Using dowel kit

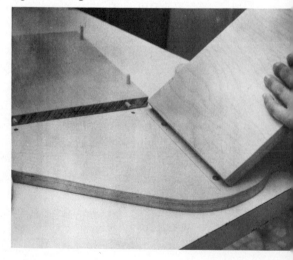

Fig. 22. Drilling before cutting design

apply glue to the insides of the dowel holes and to the edges to be joined. Insert the dowel into one piece and then force it into the matching part. If necessary, hammer the piece in place; but be sure to protect your work with a scrap of lumber when hammering so that you don't dent your work.

OTHER MEANS OF JOINING

Skilled woodworkers use a variety of joining techniques to make their work sturdier and more attractive. The more common ones—which are useful in producing boxes, drawers, shelves, and other objects—are shown under "Types of Joints" in Chapter 11. You will use some of them to produce the projects included in this book.

4 Using a scroll saw with skill and precision

For precise and intricate work, the scroll saw provides an enormous advantage over other power saws because of its thin, narrow, flexible blade. It enables you to cut short radius curves with fine kerfs, and facilitates scrollwork, fretwork, and other delicate jobs that require sharp turns of the blade.

The blade is held in place at the top and bottom and inserted with the teeth pointing toward you and downward. When cutting heavy material use wide blades with fewer teeth and feed the work slowly. Narrow blades with more and finer teeth work best for fine cutting on light stock, and the work can be fed faster. Blades do become dull, but you can prolong their life by raising or lowering the saw table so that the cutting will be done by a different section of the blade. To avoid the splintering of cut edges—which sometimes occurs on plywood—place a waste piece of wood underneath the piece you are cutting.

Work is fed into the Moto-Shop by raising the blade guard, pressing the wood up to the blade, and then releasing the guard. The guard has spring tension so that, in addition to protecting your fingers, it holds the work in place. As noted previously, Dremel's new plastic blade guard does not have to be raised manually when you are sawing thin stock. You simply press the material against it and it raises itself. The wood is usually fed into the saw with the right hand while the left hand turns and guides the work (Figure 23). This is not an inflexible rule, however. The important thing is to position your hands as comfortably as possible and to maneuver them as necessary to keep the blade on the line. Be sure your work area is well-lit so that you have no difficulty seeing the pattern lines that the blade must follow. Remember that the blade will remove material equal to its width; so to maintain accurate dimensions, saw on the outside edge of the pattern line. It's easy to sand away excess wood but there's no easy way to put it back!

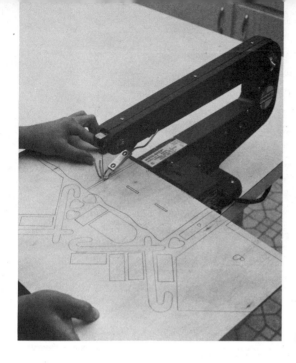

Fig. 23. Feeding work into saw

Don't force material into the saw; let the blade do the work. If you force it you may bend the blade out of line, producing an uneven cut or even breaking the blade. You may also break the blade if you attempt to make too sharp a turn. About half an inch is required for a turn that reverses the direction of the cut. Feed the work steadily, not too rapidly and not too slowly. Don't stop feeding and allow the blade to continue operating in a stationary position; it may burn the wood or produce an unsightly notch.

ANGLE CUTS

Your jigsaw will make surprisingly sharp turns but it will not make a perfect right-angle cut. These cuts and sharper angle cuts are made by making one cut to the intersection of the angle, backing the blade out of the kerf, and making another cut on the second angle (Figure 24). Occasionally, sawdust jams the kerf so that the blade will not back out. Turn off the saw and remove the obstruction with a pin, or by threading a piece of dental floss into the kerf and working it up and down. In some situations you can diverge from the pattern and cut far enough into waste wood to turn the blade around and return to the pattern line.

The table on the Moto-Shop can be tilted to make bevel cuts (Figure 25). This is accomplished by loosening the top wing nut located under the table at the front of the saw. Tilt the table until the desired angle is indicated on the calibrated scale, tighten the nut, and you are ready to go. To ensure absolute accuracy, check the angle of the cut on a piece of waste wood before cutting the work itself, and adjust the table as necessary.

Fig. 24. Making an angle cut   Fig. 25. Making a bevel cut

INTERIOR CUTS

Unlike most saws, the jigsaw will make interior cuts without a lead-in kerf. Use the flexible shaft attachment to drill a $\frac{5}{32}$-inch hole in the waste material that will be removed from the interior cut (Figure 26). Remove the blade, thread it through the hole, and replace it in the saw (Figures 27 and 28).

To save cutting time, keep the hole for blade insertion close to the cutting line. To cut square corners approach the angle from one direction, back out to the cutting hole, and then approach it from the

Fig. 26. Drilling with flexible shaft

Fig. 27. Threading blade (above right)
Fig. 28. Making interior cut (right)

other direction. If a round corner will do you can make it with a continuous cut (Figure 29).

When making objects, such as jigsaw puzzles, where the cut-out interior sections will be replaced in the frame, you may wish to avoid the hole required to thread the blade. In this case, make a lead-in cut and fill the kerf with wood filler to hold the frame together. When dry, sand it smooth.

Fig. 29. Round corner

STRAIGHT CUTS

When you become proficient with the saw you will probably be able to make accurate straight cuts freehand by simply following the pattern line. If you have trouble doing so at the outset, you can improvise a fence to guide your work (Figure 30). Cut a piece of one-by-two-inch board to fit the saw table and fasten it the correct distance from the blade with two C-clamps. Press your work against it to guide the wood through the saw. The fence can also be used to cut several pieces the same width or length and to cut dowel pegs. Set the fence the desired distance from the blade, place a square block against it, and use the block to push the dowel through the saw (Figure 31). This assures you of equal length and straight ends.

Ultimately, to make straight cuts more quickly and accurately, you may wish to invest in a table saw. In 1978 Dremel introduced a four-inch table saw only 13-inches wide, 8¾-inches high, and 11½-inches deep, that weighs only twelve pounds. It will make cross cuts in stock up to one inch (Figure 32); will rip stock one-inch thick, using a self-aligning rip fence; and can be used to cut mortise and tenon, and tongue in groove joints. The blade tilts to make bevel cuts at an angle up to forty-five degrees (Figure 33) and a miter gauge is provided to make miter cuts up to forty-five degrees (Figure 34).

Fig. 30. Improvised fence

Fig. 31. Using fence to cut dowel

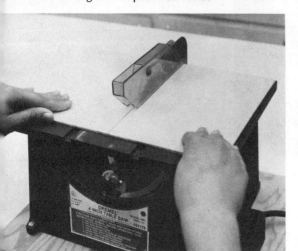

Fig. 32. Straight cut with table saw

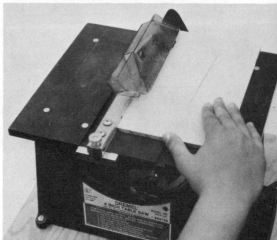

Fig. 33. Bevel cut with table saw

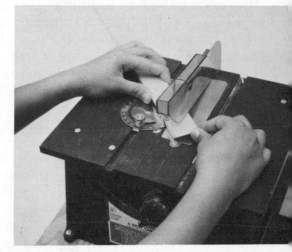

Fig. 34. Miter cut with table saw

LONG CUTS

Long cuts that exceed the fifteen-inch throat capacity of the Moto-Shop can be made by removing the blade from the forward slots and placing it in the slots on either side. This enables you to cut pieces of any length as long as they are no more than fifteen inches wide (Figure 35).

Fig. 35. Making long cut

CUTTING SMALL PIECES

Very small pieces are difficult to cut without removing the blade guard, but it is dangerous to saw them without it because your fingers are so close to the blade. You can avoid this risk by cutting small pieces from a piece of stock large enough to leave a handle to hold until the final cut. Make all of the other cuts first and then remove the piece that has served as the handle (Figures 36 and 37).

CUTTING DUPLICATE PIECES

To cut several pieces that must be precisely the same size and shape, make a "sandwich" of the required number of pieces; fasten them together with fine nails, and saw them as though they were a single piece of wood. If possible, place the nails in waste material so you won't have to fill the holes. Blocks and disks, such as those used for wheels on toys, can be made easily by cutting slices from the proper size board or dowel. If you need several one-by-one-inch blocks, set your fence one inch from the blade and cut the required number of pieces from one-by-one-inch stock.

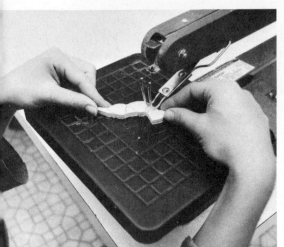

Figs. 36–37. Leaving a "handle" to cut small piece

DRILLING DELICATE PIECES

Drilling holes in delicate pieces without breaking them is sometimes difficult, particularly if you must drill with the grain of the wood. To avoid breakage drill the hole before you saw out the delicate piece (Figure 38).

APPLIED WOOD

Although the Moto-Shop will cut a standard two-by-four, it is difficult to make some cuts and keep the blade in a vertical position. It is often easier and neater to cut several thinner pieces the same shape and glue them together, sanding the edges smooth after the pieces have been glued. Thus, to make a pull toy three-inches thick, you would cut three one-inch pieces and glue them together. This process can also be used to prepare blocks for carving.

Fig. 38. Drilling delicate piece

USING THE FLEXIBLE SHAFT

Drilling, routing, drum sanding, and other operations can be accomplished with the flexible shaft on your Moto-Shop. With the switch in the "off" position attach the flexible shaft to the power takeoff. As with the saw, don't use excessive pressure; let the tool do the work. If you force it you will slow it down or even stall the motor, and it is speed, not pressure, that removes the wood. The tool is simple to operate. Hold it as you would a pencil, but to ensure firm and accurate control be sure the hand holding the tool is resting on a firm surface.

The flexible shaft is equipped with a $\frac{5}{32}$-inch twist drill that can be used to drill the hole for interior cuts. Larger dimensions should be drilled with a power drill or brace and bit. Be careful when drilling to maintain the drill in an accurate vertical position or your holes will be out of line.

5 The art of power woodcarving

Three-dimensional carving—which is really sculpting in wood—is more than a skill: It is an art that at its higher levels requires considerable artistic talent. Hammer and chisel carving, in addition to skill and dexterity, also demands a certain amount of physical strength and endurance. Thus, few among us can aspire to true artistry when working with hand tools and wood.

When Albert Dremel invented the Moto-Tool, he broadened the horizons of thousands of would-be carvers who were suddenly able to produce beautiful carvings that were beyond their grasp with hand tools.

The Moto-Tool is available in several models, ranging from constant speed devices to the rugged Model 380, which operates at variable speeds from 5,000 to 25,000 RPM. Also available is the Moto-Flex Tool, which operates at a constant speed of 25,000 RPM and is equipped with a thirty-four-inch neoprene covered flexible shaft. Many carvers, particularly women, find the handpiece on the Moto-Flex tool easier to hold and maneuver than the basic Moto-Tool. Your choice among the various options should be dictated by cost, versatility, and the amount of carving you plan to do.

The basic Moto-Tool kit includes a variety of accessories—more than enough to get you started—and an instruction manual that includes descriptions of additional accessories that increase the versatility of the tool and which can be purchased individually. Ultimately, you can equip your Moto-Tool with literally scores of useful attachments: tungsten carbide cutters, small engraving cutters, abrasive wheel points, silicon grinding points, cutting wheels, steel saws, wire brushes, bristle brushes, and polishing and sanding accessories. The manual describes precisely how each of these accessories is used so that you can select those that fit your needs.

Those considering the purchase of a Moto-Tool will be heartened to know that its utility is not limited to hobby items. It has the added virtue (when you're not using it for carving or craft projects) of being a remarkably handy gadget to perform countless tasks around the house. As Jim Mayes says in his book, *How to Make Knives,* "the Moto-Tool will do almost anything except make coffee." Once you own one you'll wonder how you ever survived without it.

The Moto-Tool manual describes fifty-eight different uses for the tool and owners are discovering new ones every day. A sample of the things the Moto-Tool can do when not in use for woodcarving includes its use to cut copper tubing or light steel rods, clean spark plugs, fit floor tile, remove rusty bolts from license plates, drill holes in plaster, clean and polish silverware, sharpen tools and chain saw blades, reslot problem screws, engrave tools, remove rust, remove old putty from windows, carve and polish gem stones, sand small interior areas, clean grooves when finishing antique furniture, and even clean the heads on your golf clubs.

Now back to woodworking, which is what this book is all about. Hold the Moto-Tool as you would a pencil, and use it in much the same way. Rest your hand and arm on a firm surface for better control of the tool and let the cutting head do the work. Don't apply much pressure; simply let the cutting head eat away the wood. Stop and inspect your work frequently and be careful not to remove too much wood. You can always remove more but you can't put any back.

As you get more deeply into carving you may wish to acquire a Moto-Tool holder, so that you will have both hands free to maneuver your work, or Dremel's D-Vise, which will adjust to almost any position and firmly hold your work. In any event, be sure the wood you are cutting is held firmly and always keep both hands behind the cutting head of the tool.

Once you get the feel of the Moto-Tool you'll find it easy to use, but don't expect too much too soon. Practice on scrap lumber with several cutting heads to learn the speed and manner in which they cut. Then begin by producing some relatively simple raised relief carvings or engravings that are simply etched into the flat surfaces of boards. Basswood and white pine are easiest to cut; hardwoods such as walnut and cherry produce a finer result.

To do an incised line carving, find an attractive pattern in a magazine or book and outline it on the wood. Then trace over the outline with a #107 engraving cutter, removing wood slowly until you have achieved an attractive depth (Figure 39). Hold the Moto-Tool at an approximate forty-five degree angle and always work from right to left.

When you have gained confidence and achieved a satisfactory result, turn to the carving section and try raised relief carving on a

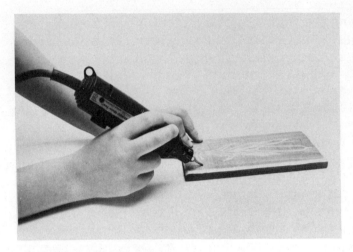

Fig. 39. Relief carving

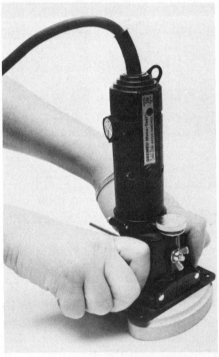

Fig. 40. Routing a base piece

plaque. Finally, when you feel you have mastered the tool, move on to some of the sculpture patterns in the book.

Don't overlook the ability of the Moto-Tool inserted in a router attachment to do beading, veining, routing, and grooving. You can use it to manufacture your own bases and plaques (Figure 40), to groove various types of joints for furniture-making, to make decorative moldings, and for most other purposes which require the routing process.

6 Selecting the right wood

A variety of materials, including acrylic plastic sheets, Masonite, and even metal can be cut with the Moto-Shop and Moto-Tool and used to fashion craft projects. With the exception of a few sample plastic and Masonite uses, most of the objects in this book are made of wood.

Your choice of material will be determined by the nature of the project. Will it be painted or finished with a clear finish that exposes the grain of the wood? Must it resist stress or support a heavy load? Is durability a requirement? Will the edges be concealed or exposed? Answer these questions and then select the least expensive material that will do the job, and the one that is easiest to work. The price of the material will vary according to the grade and scarcity of the wood.

Hardwoods, such as walnut, oak, white ash, and sugar maple, are more expensive than softwoods and more difficult to cut with the jigsaw. Softwoods, such as basswood, white or sugar pine, yellow poplar, and redwood, are less expensive and easier to cut.

Obviously, if you want to make fine furniture you will select a solid hardwood with strength and an appealing grain. Smaller painted objects that need not withstand great stress or weight can be fashioned from softer woods. Objects made of thin material will have greater strength if made from plywood.

When selecting materials, remember that some plywood has a tendency to chip at the edges when it is cut. You can save money by using cheaper plywoods, such as fir, but it really isn't worth it; the edges splinter so badly that it is difficult to produce satisfactory, finished work. On the other hand, hardwood veneers, while more expensive, provide a more attractive finished product. Before selecting the material for a project, remember that most plywood has an unattractive edge. Don't use it on projects where the edges will be exposed unless they will be covered by paint.

Before you get really involved in woodworking, take the time to learn more about the materials available in your area. Prospect the local lumber supply houses and hobby shops and inspect the materials they have available. Buy some samples and experiment with them. This will give you a feel for how they cut and help you decide which woods you prefer to use. When buying plywood, you will find some dealers who sell pieces cut to the dimensions you request. Others will demand that you buy a full, four-by-eight-foot sheet. If so, have the dealer cut it into four, two-by-four-foot pieces. The Moto-Shop is versatile, but it wasn't built to handle large sheets.

Remember that, although widths are described in inches, a two-by-four is not really two inches by four inches. Boards are planed on all surfaces before they leave the mill; so when you get the two by four it actually measures only 1¾ inches by 3⅝ inches. A one-by-two is really ¾ inches by 1⅝ inches.

Softwood is carried in grades one to three, the lowest number indicating the most nearly perfect board. Plywood is graded by letters; A is the best and it may be finished on one or both sides. The thinnest plywood is ⅛-inch, and the sizes increase in ⅛-inch intervals. The ½-inch thickness is the heaviest you are likely to use and, if it is hardwood, about the largest your saw will handle.

When buying wood don't settle for the first piece the lumber dealer shows you. Go through his stock yourself and select pieces that are as free of knots, dents, scratches, and other blemishes as possible. Don't buy pieces that are warped, cupped, or twisted.

Most of the items in this book were made of various thicknesses of basswood, white pine, and a fine quality birch plywood that is sold under the tradename "Baltic Birch." This product has more than the usual number of veneer layers, which are alternately dark and light. The edges, when finished naturally, produce an interesting and attractive design, and the plywood itself cuts cleanly, and sands smoothly.

Here are a few additional tips that you will find helpful as you work with wood:

• Save your scrap pieces of lumber and plywood. You'll find that sooner or later all but the very smallest will be put to some use.

• Store plywood sheets flat and preferably weight them down because they have a tendency to warp when standing on edge.

• Don't mix woods in a project if you plan to stain and finish them with a clear finish. All woods do not take stain the same way and you may find yourself with a botched-up project if more than one wood is used. The exception, of course, is a project that calls for contrasting woods.

• When assembling objects such as boxes, make sure that the grain on all parts runs in the same direction; it makes a more attractive finished product.

● Individual plywood parts will have greater strength if the surface grain runs with the longest dimension.

● While plywood is appropriate for most craft projects, it should usually not be used for carving. If you go through the top layer of veneer with your cutter you will probably have an unsightly result.

● Softwoods are easiest to carve but tend to yield fuzzy edges that must be sanded away. Hardwoods cut cleanly and even the toughest ones cut easily with the Moto-Tool.

● Some woods, like Douglas fir and Zebra wood, are difficult to carve cleanly. The density and hardness of the grain vary considerably, so that when you run the cutter across the grain it produces a bumpy surface by gouging more deeply into the softer grain. It also causes problems when cutting with the grain because the cutter would often rather follow the harder grain than the pattern line.

When you do relief carving you can avoid errors by going over the pattern on the wood and shading in the areas where the wood is to be removed.

7 How to make your own patterns

Patterns are supplied for most of the items in this book but don't allow yourself to be restricted by them. You can use the transfer-by-squares process to alter the dimensions of any project, adapting it to other designs, or even to create totally new designs of your own.

You can employ transfer-by-squares to enlarge or reduce any designs that you wish to copy from other sources—books, magazines, greeting cards, even fabric and wallpaper. Many people have difficulty reproducing or altering the dimensions of a design freehand. Transferring-by-squares enables them to do it accurately, one small piece at a time.

In order to make your own pattern, first draw a grid on a piece of tracing paper. Then trace a design from any source onto the grid. To enlarge or reduce the design, follow the instructions under "How to Use Patterns." Bear in mind that when you trace a design onto a $\frac{1}{2}$-inch grid and transfer it to a one-inch grid you actually increase the area of the object four times. While you can transfer a pattern from any size grid to any other, you will achieve greater accuracy if the original grid is at least $\frac{1}{4}$-inch, and if you don't attempt in one step too great an increase in size. Instead, enlarge your design once and then enlarge it again.

If both halves of the design you are copying are identical it is easier to reproduce them exactly if you trace only one-half of the design. Then fold the paper, as for half-patterns, turn it over, and trace the other half. When you unfold the paper the pattern will be complete with identical sides.

When you have completed your rough pattern go over it carefully, using guides such as rulers and French curves to refine the pattern lines. You can also use tops and cans from your kitchen for this purpose, but you'll be rewarded if you visit an art supply store and purchase a good compass and protractor and some inexpensive templates. You can get them to produce many sizes of squares, ovals, triangles, and other shapes. The French curve templates will aid you in creating your own scroll designs.

To transfer a pattern from one sheet to another or directly to the wood, use graphite rather than typewriter carbon paper; it is less apt to smear and produces a darker line. Some artists improvise graphite paper by covering the reverse side of a pattern with graphite, applied with the side of a pencil lead. When you trace over the design the graphite on the back of the pattern is transferred to the paper below.

8 Finishing your work

The projects in this book are painted, stained, or finished with a clear wood finish. Many of the painted designs may be more elaborate than some woodworkers will wish to attempt. If that's true for you, don't be put off by it. The designs that are shown represent one artist's inclinations. You are free to adapt, simplify, or alter them to suit your own skills and tastes. Many of the items will be attractive if you simply stain them or finish them in their natural color.

To finish and decorate your projects you will need a scissors, pencils, eraser, tracing paper, graphite paper, sable brushes, acrylic paints, gesso, wood stains, clear wood finish, and spray varnish made for use with acrylic paints (Figure 41).

You are not locked into the authors' selection of materials, of course. You may use the finishing materials of your choice, making sure that non-toxic paints are used, particularly on items intended for use by children. However, all of the painted projects in this book were finished with artist's acrylic paints, applied over a gesso base coat. The base colors on a few of the larger items are household acrylic enamel, sprayed with a matte finish varnish formulated for use with acrylic paint, which was then sanded lightly before the decorations were applied. Gesso is an ideal base coat for acrylics because it fills in the minor imperfections in the wood, is opaque, and provides good adhesion.

Use sable brushes of the appropriate size to apply acrylic paints, and add enough water to the paint so that it flows on with a smooth consistency. It is better to apply two or three thin coats of paint than one thick coat that reveals unsightly brush marks. Premix your colors, making sure that you have enough of each to complete the project. If you don't use all of the paint in one sitting, cover it with plastic food wrap so that it doesn't dry out before your next opportunity to use it. If you mix your paint in the lid of a margarine cup, you can use the cup as a cover.

Fig. 41. Finishing supplies

Before you begin finishing a project, check the surface one last time to be sure it is free of defects and satin smooth. Fill nicks and scratches with plastic wood, let it dry, and do a final sanding with extra fine abrasive paper (Figure 42). Apply a gesso base coat (two if needed) and be sure it covers well (Figure 43). Sand it lightly to remove brush marks, lumps, and other imperfections. Now trace the design onto the gesso-covered surface. You can do this by using graphite paper or by scratching a layer of pencil lead on the reverse side of the pattern, and then tracing over the design (Figure 44). Now paint in the design details (Figure 45) and then the background. (Some artists prefer to cover the entire surface with the background color before applying the pattern, and paint the design details last.) Spray the finished product with acrylic spray varnish when the paint is thoroughly dry (Figure 46).

Fig. 42. Final sanding

Fig. 43. Applying gesso

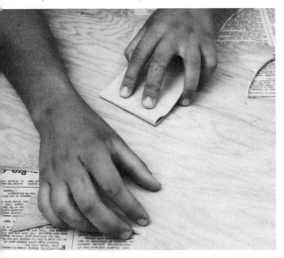

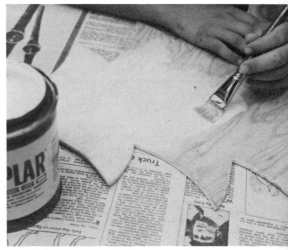

Fig. 44. Transferring design

Fig. 45. Painting in design

If you want to finish the projects precisely as shown, determine the colors by referring to the color photographs included on the covers and elsewhere in the book. Otherwise, pick your own favorite colors or alter colors on household items to match your own home's decor.

Acrylic paints are quite bright and in some applications can be given added dimension and character by antiquing, which tones the colors down. Spray the painted surface with an acrylic matte spray varnish and let it dry. Then brush on an oil paint mixture that is about three parts burnt umber to one part black, and dilute the mixture with turpentine to the consistency of nail polish. Finally, wipe off this finish with a soft cloth until you have removed enough of the antique stain

Fig. 46. Completed project

to achieve the desired effect. Complete the project by adding another coat of varnish.

Carved items and other projects that are designed to have a natural finish may be stained to duplicate various wood colors, and to enhance the grain of the wood. Apply the stain with a cloth or brush and wipe off the excess after the desired color has been obtained. The more stain you apply and the longer you leave it on the wood, the darker the wood will become. After the stain has dried, a light sanding may be required because staining tends to raise the grain of the wood. Be careful not to sand too much because it will remove some stain and may create light spots on the wood. Use an extra fine 600 grade wet/dry sandpaper dipped in water to avoid scratching the surface. After staining, apply at least three coats of sealer, sanding lightly between each coat. The more coats you apply the more the quality of the finish will be improved.

The carved items in the book were finished with Deft clear wood sealer, but other quality brands are available. Seal painted items after they are completely dry by using a spray varnish formulated for use with acrylic paints.

9 A word about creativity

"Take an object. Do something to it. Do something else to it. Do something else to it."

That's a lesson in creativity from the notebooks of the noted artist, Jasper Johns. It is one you can use to develop your own creative instincts, and one that applies to many of the designs that were created for this book.

Almost everything you see in your daily life can be a source of inspiration to stimulate your creative imagination. Wallpaper is simply a room decoration until you study it creatively and determine other uses to which its design can be put. The drawings in a child's coloring book may, with a bit of ingenuity, provide suitable patterns for ornaments, toys, and other objects.

This book should inspire you to do more than reproduce the designs it contains. Study the cutting and decorating patterns and then look for sources of patterns of your own creation. Consider what you can do with a single pattern by altering its size. The "Rocking Horse" pattern, for example, has been used to produce a three-inch Christmas ornament and another version large enough to hold a child. You might adapt it further by simply cutting the horse's head, attaching a three-foot piece of ¾-inch dowel, and placing a 1½-inch wooden knob on the other end. The "Rocking Horse" has now become a hobby horse.

Literally dozens of the patterns—such as those on "Noah's Ark," the "Cookie Cutter Christmas Tree," and the "Nativity Mobile"—can be used as patterns for Christmas tree ornaments.

Most of those who protest that they are not creative underestimate their own innate talents. Creative thought processes can be developed if you try. Hopefully, this book will stimulate many of its readers to do what the authors did and what Jasper Johns suggests. Observe more closely the things around you and you may surprise yourself. You are almost certain to come up with some new craft ideas of your own!

10 Profiting from your fun

When Irving Langmuir won the Nobel prize for chemistry in 1932 he was quoted as saying, "Everything I have ever done I have done for the fun of it." Nevertheless, his fun yielded a productive career. Most light-weight power tools are sold to home hobbyists and crafts enthusiasts who use them to pursue some leisure time activity for their own amusement. That's reason enough, but many woodworkers find that their fun can yield a profit as well.

The story is told of the department store buyer who visited Tahiti and was negotiating with a native wood-carver for the purchase of fifty tikis. The native said that the first one would cost two thousand Tahitian francs.

"What about the rest?" asked the buyer.

The wood-carver pondered for a moment and replied, "Each of them will be three thousand francs."

The startled buyer, accustomed to quantity discounts, protested, "But why should they cost more?"

Smiling, the wood-carver replied, "Because the first one is fun!"

If your temperament is such that you enjoy making one of something, but can't bring yourself to do another, you probably will not want to mass produce the items you design. In that case, you wouldn't even consider going into business for yourself, as many woodworkers have done. Many men and women earn extra money by selling the projects that they design and create. It is not uncommon for a really productive artisan to earn several hundred dollars a week.

There are many outlets for handcrafted wood items. They can be marketed at crafts fairs, boutiques, and handicraft shops, and even sold directly to department stores. Many of the larger stores have sections that feature hand-crafted items purchased from local artists and artisans. In most areas of the country there are also handicraft shops that sell the same items, either purchasing them outright or accepting them for consignment sale. Some cities also permit crafts-men to sell their wares from sidewalk displays.

Fig. 47. Advertising a puppet show   Fig. 48. Menu holder

Other budget conscious jigsaw and carving buffs use their equipment to cut their costs, rather than enhance their income. Here are some other cost-conscious ways in which jigsaws and power carvers have been used:

● Elementary school teachers and art instructors enrich their programs at little cost by using scroll saws to produce games and puzzles that serve as teaching aids, and to make displays that will stimulate their pupils. Saws are also used by Boy and Girl Scout leaders, day camp counselors, and art therapists in hospitals and psychiatric institutions.

● Little theater groups, churches, and other organizations use jigsaws to construct their own props and advertising displays (Figures 47 and 48).

● Miniature and model builders use the Moto-Shop, Moto-Tool, and Moto-Lathe to fashion parts they need, or to cut the elements of original models that they design. Others use them to construct furniture for doll houses and even for their homes.

● Many women, dismayed by the prices charged for wooden toys, save substantially by producing sturdy wooden toys, games, and puzzles of their own design. If half a dozen, ten-dollar toys are produced from a couple of dollars worth of wood, a jigsaw has virtually paid for itself.

Individually crafted jigsaw and power carver projects make handsome but inexpensive gifts. The recipients appreciate receiving original designs that you have troubled to make for them yourself. You give the item knowing that it won't be a duplicate of something they already have or will receive.

How many enjoyable hobbies can you think of that have the potential of paying for themselves?

11 General instructions for projects

The projects that follow have been organized to introduce you to a variety of woodworking techniques. The range of projects is enormous and will appeal to every age and interest. They are grouped under headings that will help you choose projects that suit your particular interests. Few readers will attempt to do all of the projects in order. However, you should do enough of them to gain experience with each of the basic techniques before tackling the more difficult projects, which come later in the book.

Full-size patterns or half-patterns have been provided where possible. Other patterns must be extended in length, as indicated on the drawings. Patterns (which have been reduced) for some of the larger items will have to be enlarged by using the transfer-by-squares process. Unless otherwise specified, enlarge all squares to $\frac{1}{2}$" × $\frac{1}{2}$". In order to produce accurate work, it is important that transfers be done carefully and that instructions be followed faithfully.

Material requirements are listed only on the more complicated projects or when they are not obvious. We have included basic reference material and a legend to aid you in using the patterns.

LEGEND*

Fold   — — — — — —

Hidden lines   •••••••••   — — — — — —

Break lines   ——————/ /——————

Paint area   ▨

Placement   — — — - - — — — - - —

Join

Dimensions |←——————   ——————→|

Wood filler   ⊠

More than one piece

*These symbols are used unless otherwise indicated.

TYPES OF JOINTS

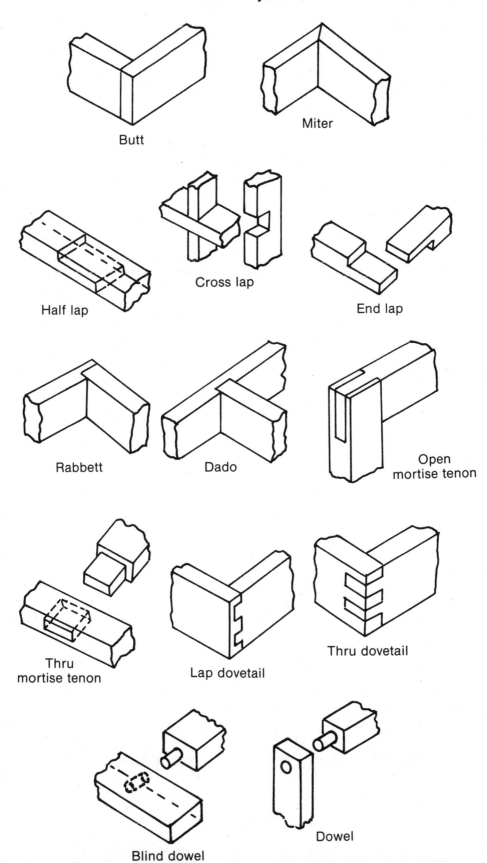

Butt

Miter

Half lap

Cross lap

End lap

Rabbett

Dado

Open
mortise tenon

Thru
mortise tenon

Lap dovetail

Thru dovetail

Blind dowel

Dowel

12 Beginner scroll saw projects

SIMPLE TOYS AND JIGSAW PUZZLES

An easy beginner project. Simple shapes traced from coloring books. Fun standup toys cut from scraps of 1" pine or basswood. Drill holes for eyes.

When using these patterns cut jigsaw puzzles from ¼" solid stock, or increase size of pattern, transferring by squares, and cut from thicker material. Remember, when cutting jigsaw puzzles, if you have difficulty following the pattern line, don't try to correct an error; keep going and improvise. No two puzzles will ever be alike. Sand outside edges of jigsaw puzzles before cutting them apart. Then sand very lightly between pieces so that they interlock freely.

Finish project according to general instructions on sanding and finishing. If puzzles are cut from thick wood and are intended to stand up, sand bottom until you are sure it is flat *before* cutting individual puzzle pieces. It's hard to do after pieces have been separated.

WARNING: All children's toys should be finished with nontoxic materials.

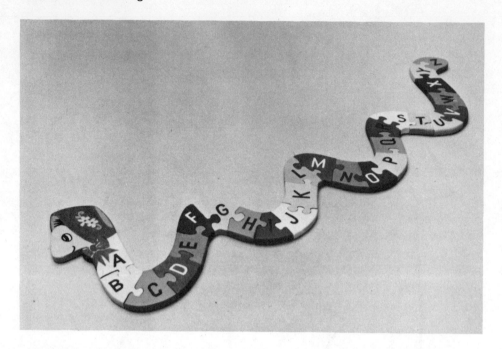

ALPHABET WORM

Learning the alphabet is fun with this colorful teaching aid. When children have mastered it they can turn it over and try to match up the blank side. It can be cut from ¼" plywood or enlarged and cut from thicker solid stock for an easy-to-handle puzzle for very small children. Finish as desired, or follow color photograph.

To cut the puzzle from two pieces of wood, trace the pattern on the first section through the letter M. Trace on second piece the pattern from L to Z. Cut out both patterns on outer line only. Separate pieces A–J and O–Z. Place one L–M section on top of the other and nail together. Cut the dividing line between L and M. Remove nails and cut the remaining pieces. This will give you a perfect fit between the two sections.

Note: See color photo on page 1 of insert.

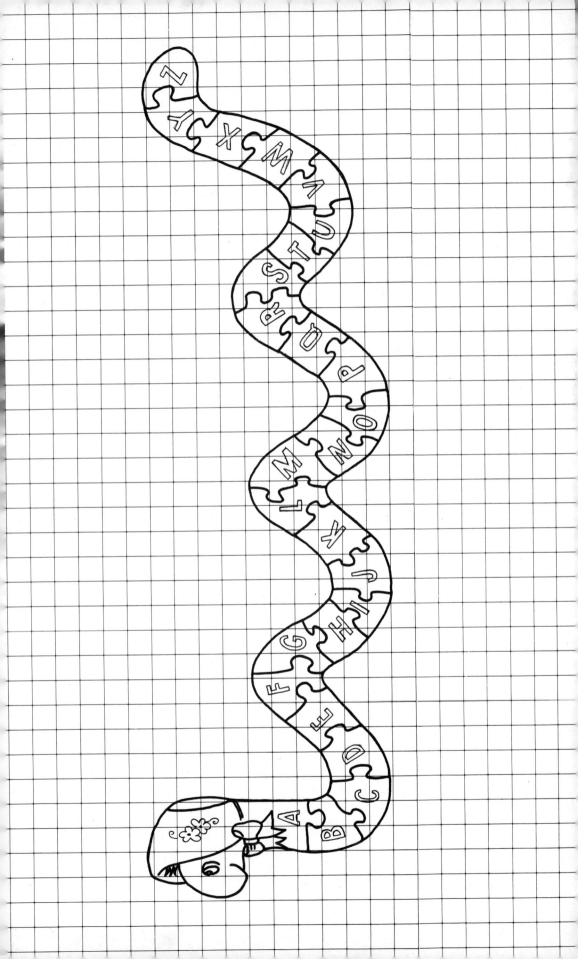

DIAMONDS AND CLOVER

A simple toy that's fun to assemble into an endless variety of interesting shapes. Enlarge half-pattern; cut from ⅛" birch plywood; sand and finish with clear wood sealer, or paint pieces a variety of bright colors. Refer to chapter 4 for instructions on cutting inside angles of interlocking slots.

Note: See color photo on page 1 of insert.

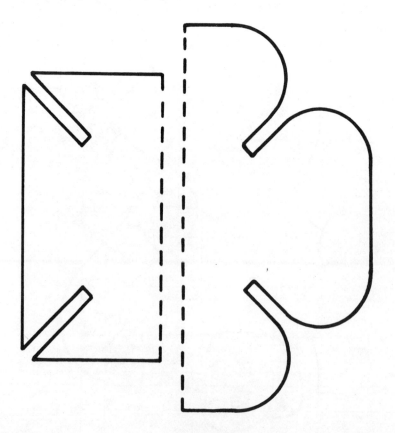

ACROBATS (the more the merrier)

These interlocking blocks will stack right-side-up, upside-down, and sideways. Cut from 1" pine or basswood. It would be nice to lay the pattern out like a jigsaw puzzle, but the pieces must be cut individually because of the right-angle cuts. Create a game by painting them as sets of twins, changing costume colors, moustaches, or other details so that the pieces can be used for a match-up game. Care must be taken to make sure that all straight cuts *are straight,* or the mini-men may not balance.

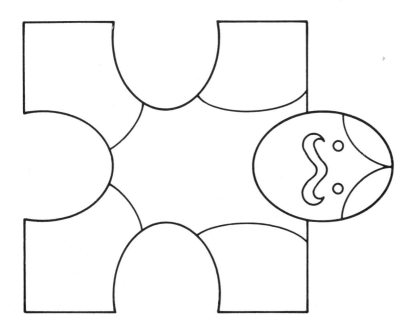

DOGHOUSE PUZZLE

This simple puzzle for a very small child is cut from ½" basswood. To make the inside cuts, drill 5⁄32" entrance holes at the lower left corner of the doghouse and on the dog's nose, using the flexible shaft on your Moto-Shop or any other drill. Drill hole for dog's eye. Sand well with sanding disk or by hand. Round off sharp corners. Finish with clear wood sealer, or paint as desired with acrylic paint.

Note: See color photo on page 5 of insert.

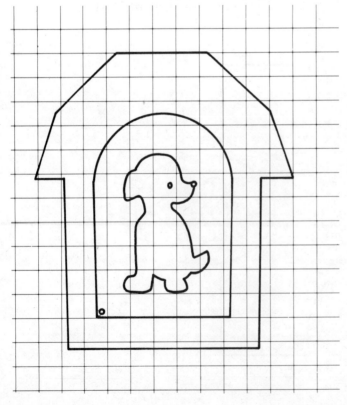

FILIGREE ORNAMENTS (can also be used as jewelry)

Cut from ⅛" birch plywood. Drill holes for string and entry holes for all inside cuts before you start sawing. Make all interior cuts before cutting outline. Begin with "Noel" and "Joy" ornaments and proceed to more delicate items.

You will learn from experience that care must be taken when cutting delicate pieces. On outer cuts, hold a piece of wood on top of the cut design to protect it while sawing the outer edge. Note the difference between the patterns and the finished ornaments. Cut first as indicated by the pattern, and then make further cuts to the degree of delicacy that your skill allows. Reduce thickness of outside outline by sanding carefully on Moto-Shop disk sander.

TAKE-APART AIRPLANE

The toy airplane on the right is an enlargement of the Christmas ornament on the left. Use pattern with "Christmas Ornaments" and transfer by squares to a ¾" grid. Toy version is made from ⅜" birch plywood; so be sure to cut slots where parts join to accommodate this dimension.

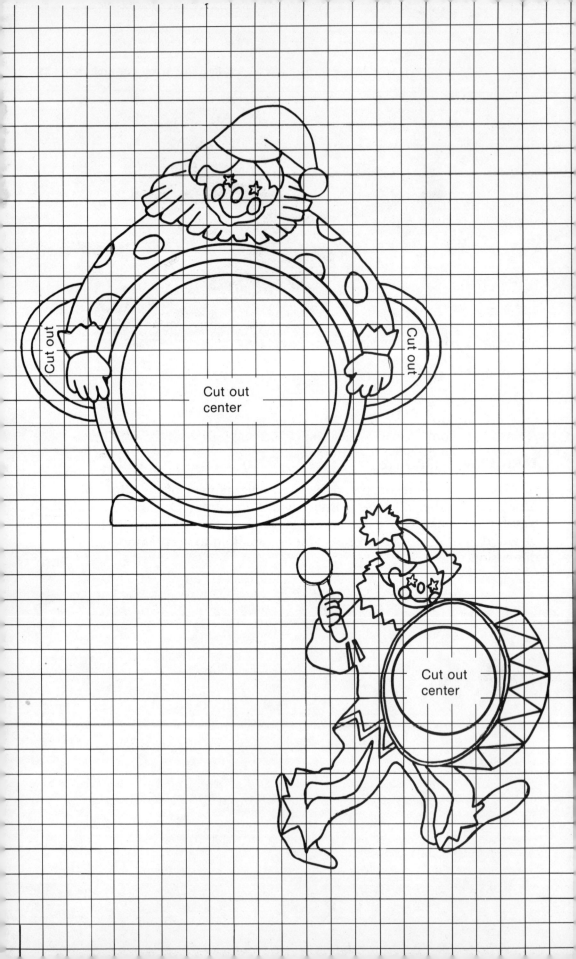

Cut out

Cut out

Cut out
center

Cut out
center

CLOWN CUP AND DISH HOLDERS

Meals will be more fun and spills less frequent with these holders for a child's cup and dish. Size of opening can be adjusted to fit your dishes. Cut from 1" basswood. They also make nice toys for baby to play with while dinner is being prepared.

See color photo on page 3 of insert.

ID TAGS

Make your own distinctive ID tags for use on luggage, key chains, etc., using ⅜" plywood. Trace your own patterns from any source. Transportation designs cut from thicker solid stock make interesting preschool toys.

SPECIAL OCCASION PLAQUES

These plaques are great for calling attention to special occasions. Greet the kids with a "Trick or Treat" door hanging on Halloween, or wish a friend a happy birthday with the "Oh Happy Day" wall hanging. All of the plaques shown are cut from ¼" plywood. They are good projects for practicing interior.

Note: See color photo on page 1 of insert.

Cat Memo Board made by enlarging an ornament pattern

COOKIE-CUTTER CHRISTMAS TREE

Materials:

Plywood $\frac{1}{4}$": 2' × 3'
Ten cookie cutters
Ten small L-hooks

Bring Christmas into your kitchen with this useful cookie-cutter holder. Enlarge half-pattern and complete it, including painting-pattern for trim and bow. Note that bow is different on the right side. It is not necessary to trace the ornaments. They are shown only to indicate placement. Cut out tree. Use full-size patterns to trace and paint ornaments directly on the tree. Punch holes in sides of cutters, so they will hang straight, and install hooks. If your cookie cutters are of a different shape, create your own designs to fit what you have.

The cookie-cutter designs can also be cut individually from $\frac{1}{8}$" plywood to hang on this tree or on your real one. Also pictured are two larger items made by tracing two of the patterns onto $\frac{1}{4}$" grids, transferring to $1\frac{1}{2}$" grids, and cutting from $\frac{1}{4}$" plywood.

Note: See color photo on page 1 of insert.

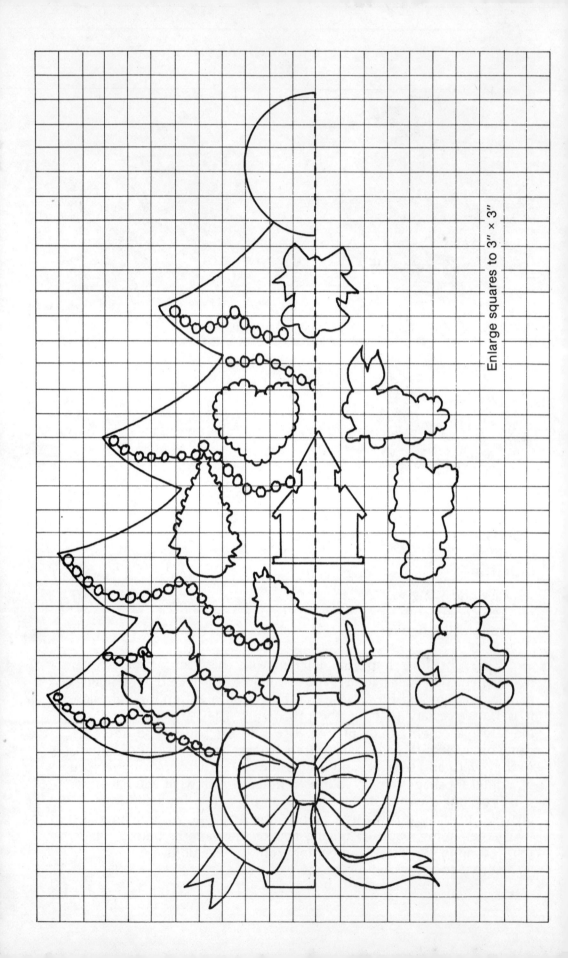

Enlarge squares to 3" × 3"

TAPE DISPENSER

This novel holder for transparent tape is cut from $\frac{1}{4}$" plywood. It will hold 300" or 400" rolls of Scotch transparent tape. Place dowels as shown in diagram. Drill shallow holes on inside of pieces to receive $\frac{7}{8}$" and $\frac{1}{8}$" dowels. Glue them in place on one side. Drill hole through other side and into large dowel for screw. Length of dowels will be determined by the width of tape you prefer.

Cut two

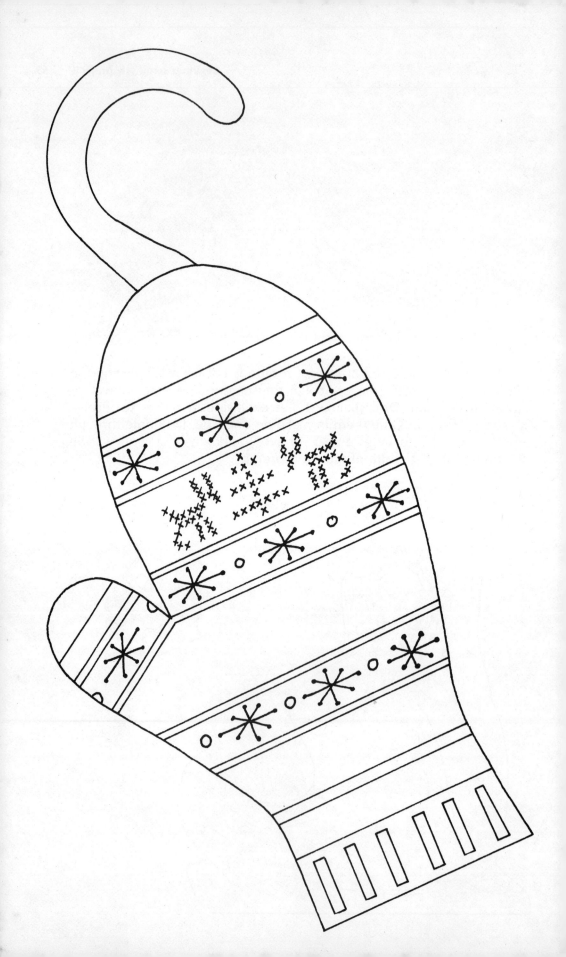

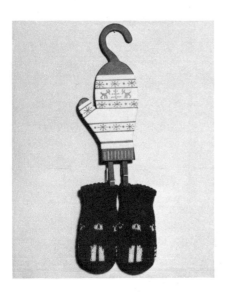

MITTEN HOLDER

Your children's mittens will always be dry if you encourage them to hang them up with this simple but attractive mitten holder. Hang it on a coat hook or doorknob. Trace pattern on ¼″ plywood; cut it out and paint. When finished glue two snap clothespins to back of holder.

DESK NAME PLATES

Cut name and base from standard one-by-two board (which won't be 1″ × 2″; see chapter 4). Drill ⅜″ hole for pencil, as shown in illustration.

Option: Make a jigsaw puzzle which, when assembled, serves as a name plate.

FLOWER POT

Trace pattern on ⅝" basswood, and drill ⅜" holes in flower and leaves, as shown, before cutting them out: It's easier to work with flat edges, unless you use a vice. Cut five graduated circles from same stock (diameters: 4", 3", 2½", 2", 1¾"), and drill ⅜" holes in centers. Enlarge holes slightly with rasp or sandpaper until they slide easily over a ⅜" dowel. Cut a ⅝" × 4" × 4" base and drill a ⅜" dowel hole in center. Cut desired length of dowel for stem, and glue into base. Item can also be made as a decorative flower pot by eliminating the base and gluing all the parts together.

Drill holes before
cutting out patterns

NUMBER SORTER BOARD

Numbers are ¼″ plywood, with ⁵⁄₁₆″ holes drilled before cutting. Base is 1″ × 4″ × 12″ solid stock. Lay numbers on board, spaced at ½″ intervals, to mark location of ¼″ dowel holes. Cut fifteen pieces of ¼″ dowel, 2¼″ long, and glue in place. Numbers can also be used as wall decorations (see photo of cradle gym).

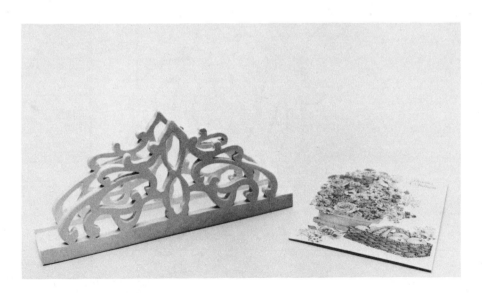

LETTER OR TOWEL HOLDER

Use ¼″ plywood with 1″ × 8″ base for letters and 4½″ × 8″ base for guest towels.

CHRISTMAS GREETINGS

Unusual holiday decoration or conversation piece for mantel or coffee table. Transfer pattern to $\frac{3}{8}$" plywood, joining letters S, T, and M in straight vertical line, as illustrated. Base is cross lap; cut second piece reversing slot, as shown.

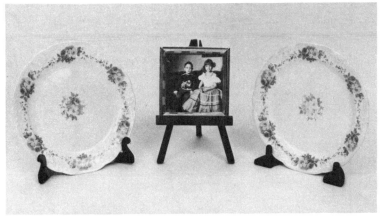

EASEL AND PLATE HOLDERS

Dowel Plateholder: Base of ¼″ solid stock. Pegs of ⁵⁄₁₆″ dowel (one piece 6″, two pieces 1″).

Easel: Tripod and shelf bottom of ¼″ plywood. Shelf front of ⅛″ plywood. Assemble tripod as shown. Glue shelf parts together and to tripod as illustrated. Join shelf and back leg with fine chain.

Filigree Plateholder: Miter vertical joint 45° and glue.

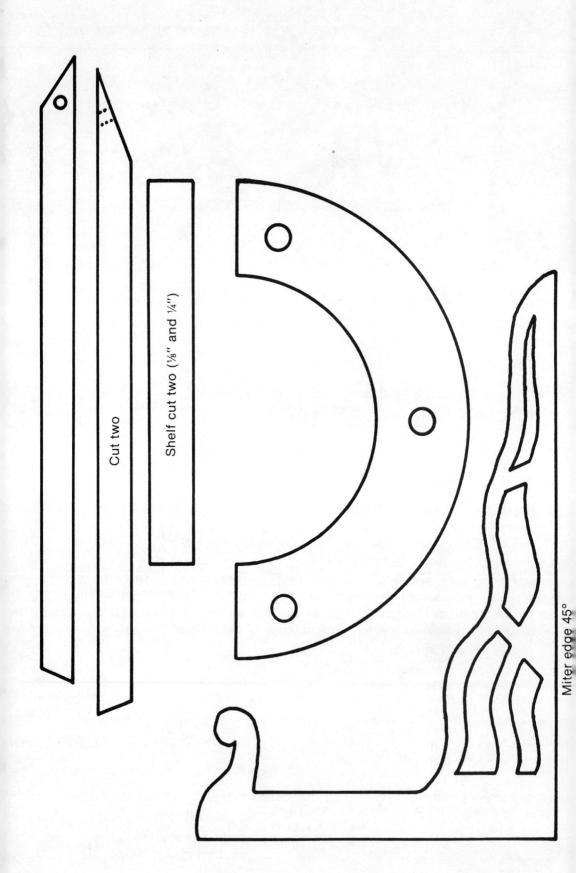

Cut two

Shelf cut two (⅛" and ¼")

Miter edge 45°

13 Applied pieces

BEDROOM DOOR PLAQUE

For your favorite teenager or little one, apply cartoon or coloring book characters to their initial. Or, if you're ambitious, spell the child's entire name on the bedroom wall. Use double stick tape to fasten letter to bedroom door.

This is a simple example of the use of applied pieces to achieve a dimensional effect that will add interest to this and other projects. Use ¼" plywood.

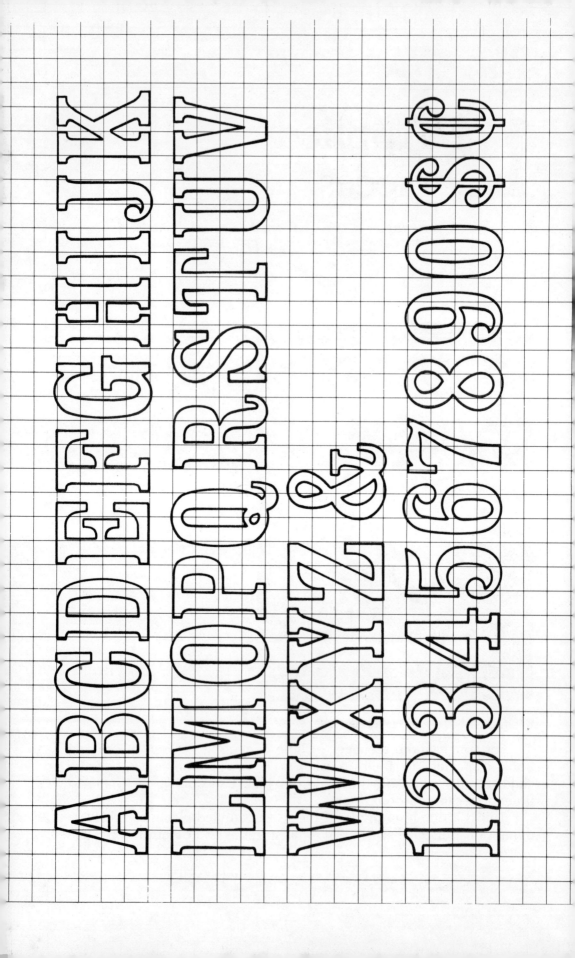

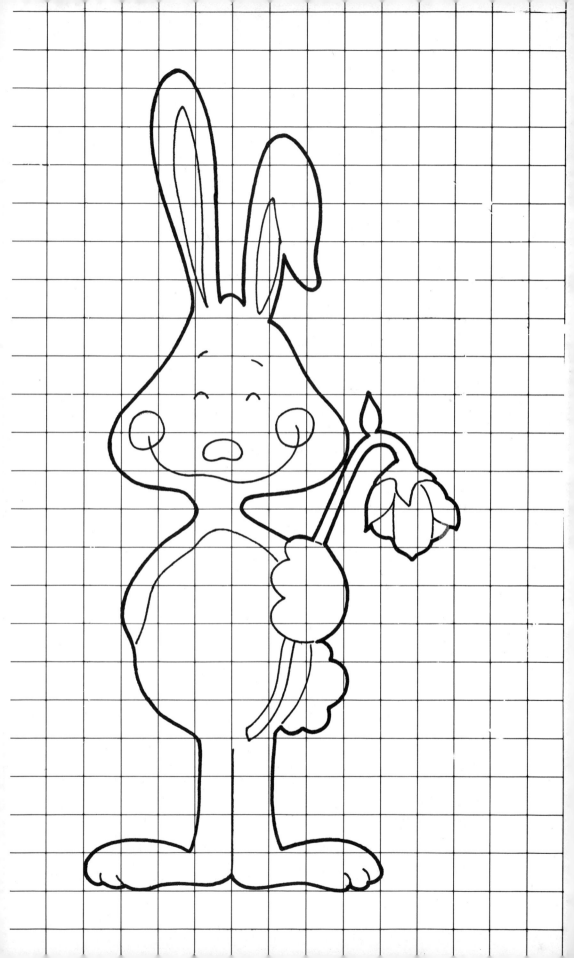

SILHOUETTE PUZZLE

Use this easy project to experiment with a different material—$\frac{1}{8}$" tempered Masonite—which cuts easily but is rather dirty. Cut two pieces, 7" × 10". Transfer pattern to the smooth surface of one piece, using white dressmaker's tracing paper. Make lead-in cut to back of heel, and cut out figure. Then cut on other lines. Glue border piece to base piece, and fill lead-in kerf with dark-colored wood filler. Apply gesso, sand, and paint board white and figure black. Replace pieces of cut-out figure to form simple jigsaw puzzle.

You don't have to use this pattern. Pick your own design from a magazine or other source; trace the outline and you have your pattern. Or do a silhouette of one of your children. Tape a piece of white paper to a wall, and have your child stand between paper and a bright, direct light. Trace around the profile shadow on the paper. Use the transfer-by-squares process to reduce the design to the desired size.

This project demonstrates the use of a lead-in cut for situations in which you don't want to mar your work with the hole required to thread the saw blade for an inside cut. It is most desirable on applied pieces because the repaired kerf will not be subjected to stress.

Note: See color photo on page 5 of insert.

OVAL PORTRAIT FRAME

Make this frame to display a cherished portrait on your desk or dressing table. Cut three pieces of ⅛" plywood to 5" × 6". Trace solid line pattern on one piece, and nail the three pieces together, placing nails inside the oval.

Cut around outer edge of pattern, sand edges, and then remove nails. Cut out center oval from top piece. Cut oval in center piece ½" larger than front opening. Cut glass or clear plastic, and picture, to fit oval. Glue sections together, or use decorative screws in center of flower designs if you want the portrait to be removable. Cut stand, miter top edge to 60° angle and glue to back of frame, or install wall hanger.

You can use the transfer-by-squares process to enlarge pattern to any size.

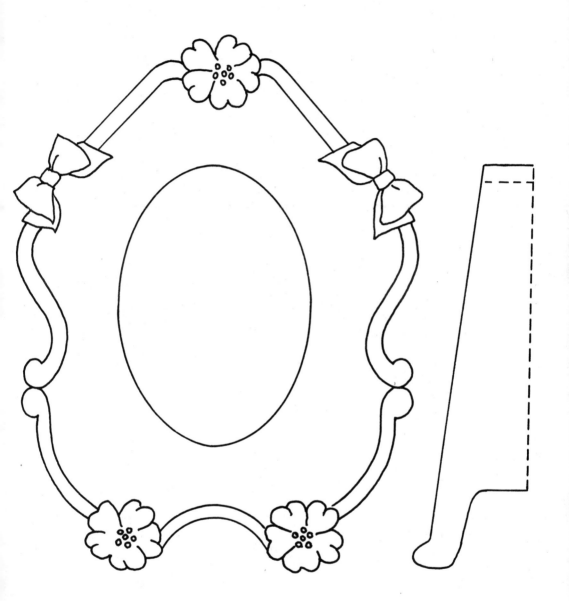

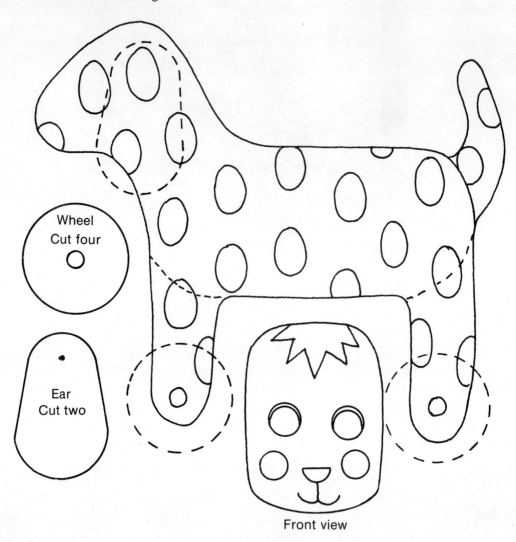

Wheel
Cut four

Ear
Cut two

Front view

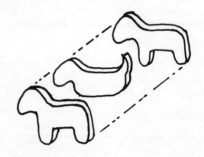

DOG PULL TOY

This toy and the next one demonstrate the principle of lamination to create objects of any thickness. Lamination will provide added dimension to your projects. Three pieces of ½" pine of two different shapes are glued together to form a dog with four legs and a perfectly centered tail. Before cutting, drill ¼" dowel holes in wheels, and 5/16" dowel holes in legs. Cut three sections as shown in diagram; assemble and glue as indicated. Run ¼" × 2¼" dowels through legs, and attach wheels with glue. Add pull string, and beads if desired. This pattern can be enlarged, using transfer-by-squares, to any size.

Note: See color photo on page 5 of insert.

RACE CAR

Three pieces of 1" pine are glued together to form this toy. The outer pieces are identical, and the figure of the driver is added to the center piece. Install 1" pine wheels with two pieces of ¼" × 3" dowel, and spare wheel with a ¼" × 1¼" piece. Drill 5/16" holes through car for axles.

Note: See color photo on page 3 of insert.

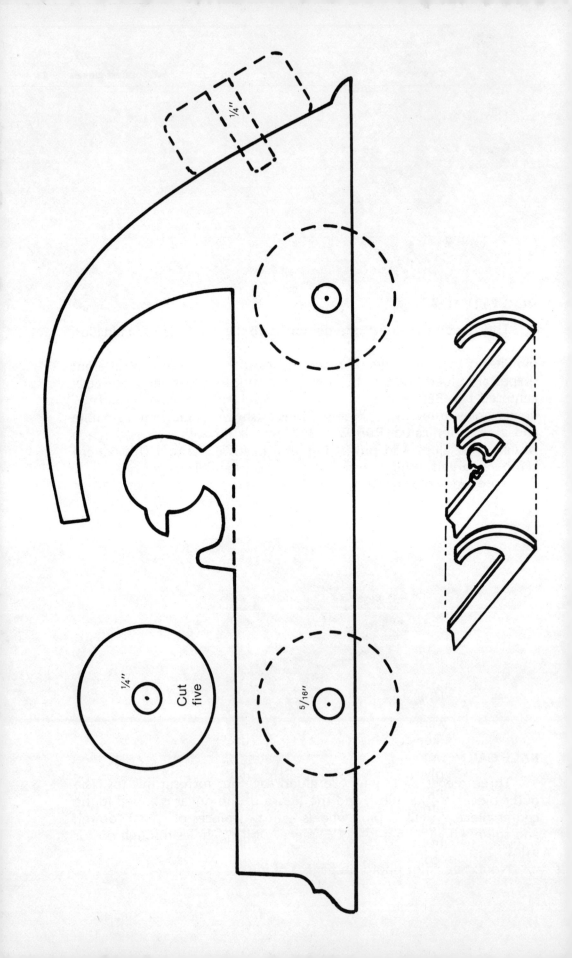

¼"

¼"

Cut
five

5/16"

THANKSGIVING PLAQUE

Here's a warm and cheerful Thanksgiving wall hanging that you might like to keep up all year 'round. Cut applied pieces from ⅛″ plywood. To make plaque (approximately 6″ × 21″), place applied pieces on ¼″ plywood, spaced ¼″ apart. Draw ¼″ border around the layout, following the curves at top and bottom. Apply gesso, and paint background before transferring designs. Refer to color illustration as guide to painting. Glue finished pieces in place as shown in illustration, and weight them until glue is thoroughly dry.

Note: See color photo on page 2 of insert.

Top and bottom pattern—Cut two

Center pattern—Cut two

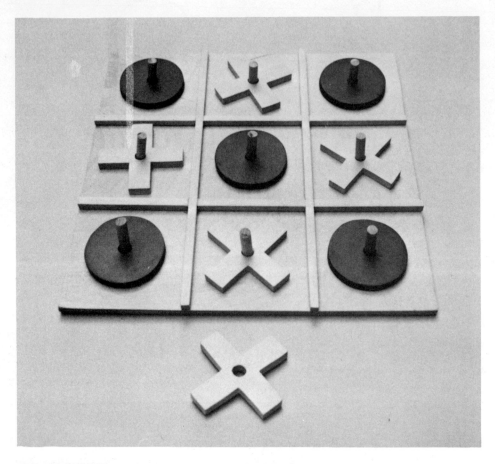

TIC-TAC-TOE

Here's a pencil and paper saver. For a variation, try playing it backward—avoid getting three in a row. Cut parts from ¼" plywood, including a 9½" × 9½" base. Use pattern as guide to locate dowel holes and slots for cross lap. Glue cross-lap strips and dowels in place. This is a good table-saw project. Set fence to rip strips and lower blade to cut half-lap slots. The nicest thing about homemade games is that you can always replace lost pieces.

Note: See color photo on page 2 of insert.

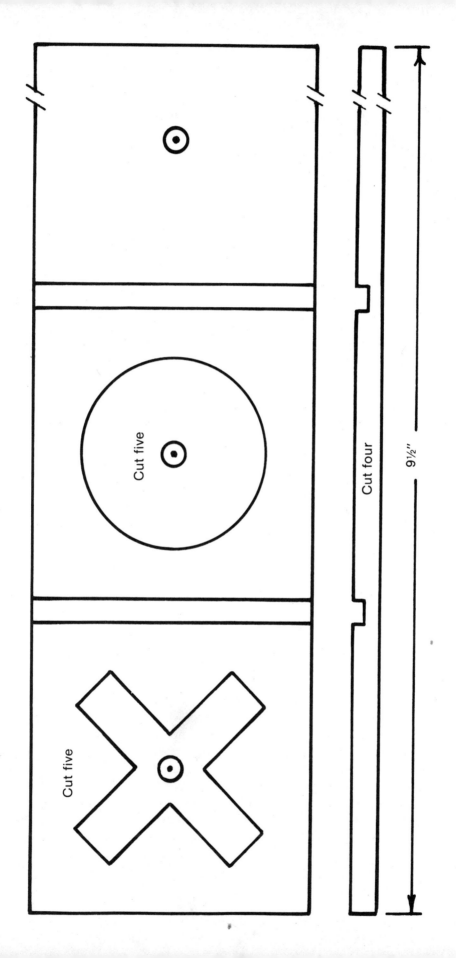

Cut five

Cut five

Cut four

9½"

14 Containers

CONTAINERS

Once you have learned the techniques for making boxes, you can produce them in any size or shape. They make unique packages for gifts that will be appreciated. Box-type construction is also employed in many other ways, although it may not always be recognized as such. This is true of many of the projects in this book.

Square or rectangular boxes can be constructed with butt or mitered corners. Butt joints are the simplest and least attractive; mitered joints are more difficult but provide a more finished appearance.

Pictured is a box with butt joints containing a puzzle (the pattern for the game is also included) that was made on the jigsaw. When your need is simply for a container, butt joints are adequate. You can make simple, inexpensive replacements for the flimsy cardboard containers in which most purchased games are packaged. When appearance is important, use mitered corners like those in the pictured gift box. Tops can be made like this one, with a mitered cover that fits over an inside liner, or more simply by applying a second piece of wood to the bottom of the cover that fits into the box.

Round boxes can be made by cutting matching disks of wood for the top and bottom, and one or more rings of the same size which can be glued together to form a box of any depth. Boxes may be stained, or painted and decorated to appear gift-wrapped. Here's a bow to begin your gift-wrapping.

Note: See color photos on pages 2 and 5 of insert.

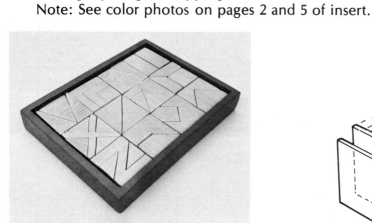

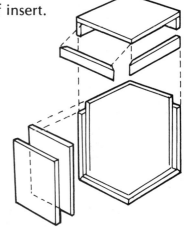

¾" pine

BUTTERFLY BOX AND SNOWMAN BOX

Boxes with irregular shapes can be made with sides that align with their tops (e.g., butterfly box), or with recessed sides with the same or similar shape (e.g., snowman box). To make the butterfly box, nail two pieces of ⅛" plywood and one piece of 1" pine together, with the ⅛" pieces on the outside. Trace pattern on top piece and cut all three simultaneously. Remove nails and place side pattern on 1" pine piece.

Drill entrance hole for sawblade inside the inner line of the "side" pattern. Saw inside line and discard waste. Make entry cut to remaining pattern line and saw around it. Close entry kerf in inside piece by gluing. Mark pieces to be sure that they remain in original position while assembling the box, or they may not fit. Sand pieces carefully, and glue outer sides to box top and inner sides to bottom.

The snowman box is made the same way, but the sides are recessed and their shape simplified, so the center piece is cut separately. To make a standup container for holly or candy canes, cut two sides and a bottom of any depth, and substitute it for the triangular sides.

Note: See color photo on page 2 of insert.

Cut two

Top
and bottom
—Cut two

Side pattern

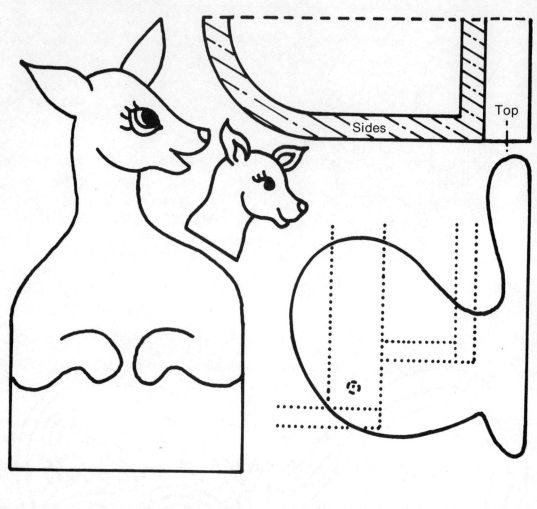

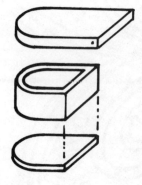

KANGAROO BOX

Box bottom, kangaroos, and legs are cut from ¼" plywood; box top from ½" pine; sides from 1" pine. Glue and nail body to back edge of box top. Glue small kangaroo to box top. Cut box sides and glue to bottom. Glue assembled box between legs. Line up box top with the front of box (top will overhang at back). Place nails for hinges in projecting back of box top, as shown in diagram.

Note: See color photo on page 2 of insert.

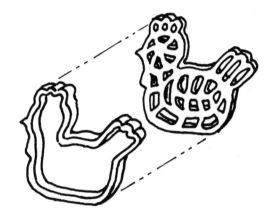

EGG HOLDER OR TRIVET

A plaque to hang on your kitchen wall—
Or a nifty trivet; but that's not all.
When you cook, put your eggs inside
So off the counter they won't slide.

Trace design on a ¼" piece of solid stock, and place on top of ½" piece. Nail together through spaces that will be removed. Cut out and sand edges. Drill blade-entry holes through openings in base and partway into piece below. Remove nails and cut openings in base. Cut rim from ½" piece; sand; glue pieces together and weight them until glue is dry. If you make the trivet for a gift or bazaar item, attach the poem.

Note: See color photo on page 3 of insert.

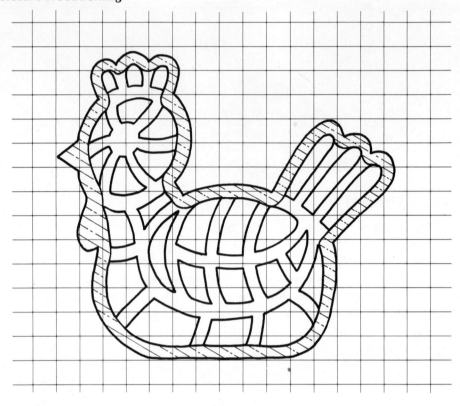

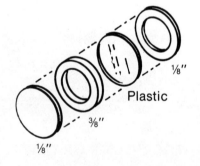

1/8"

Plastic

3/8"

1/8"

SPORTS GAMES

Before assembling games, gesso and paint background on base. Transfer pattern to base, and drill shallow depressions for the steel balls, using a #107 cutter on the Moto-Tool or a $5/32$" drill on the flexible shaft of the Moto-Shop. Paint detail, and gesso and paint remaining inside surfaces and the top of the top ring. Glue side ring to base and insert required number of small metal balls. Add plastic top and secure top ring with nails. Sand outside surfaces smooth, gesso and paint.

Note: See color photo on page 2 of insert.

PIGGY BANK

Cut five pattern pieces from solid stock—two outer pieces and center piece from ¼" and other two pieces from ½". Cut two or more at a time, as skill allows. Grid pattern is included to provide painting detail and to facilitate an increase in size if desired. Glue together per diagram. On this and other applied projects, sand edges carefully after gluing to remove ridges caused by sawing variations. Coarse Disston Abrader may be needed before sanding by hand or with drum sander on Moto-Tool.

Note: See color photo on page 3 of insert.

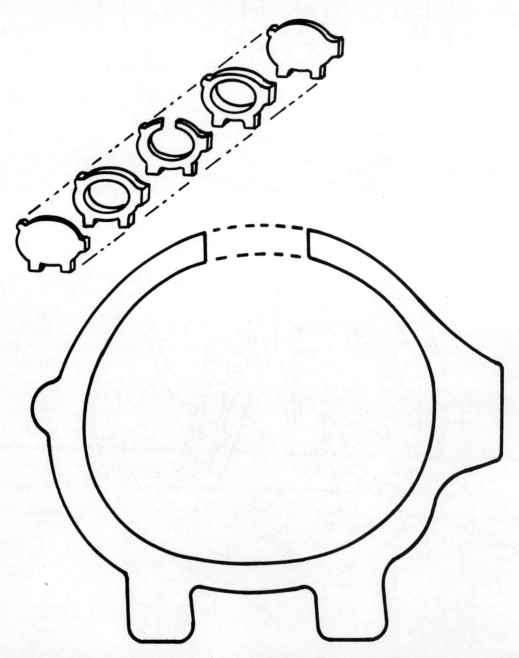

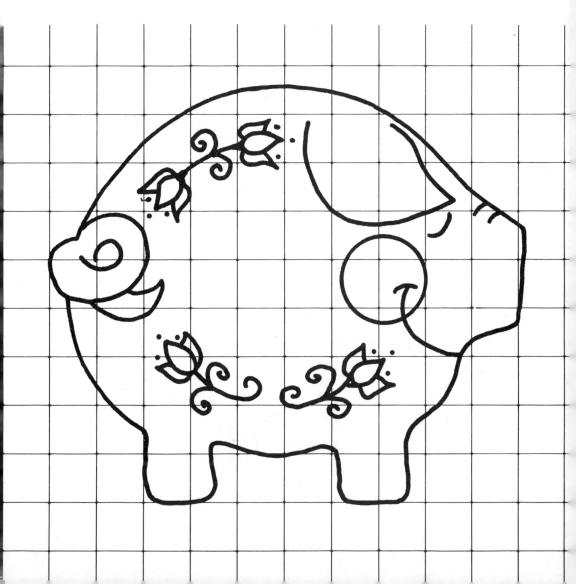

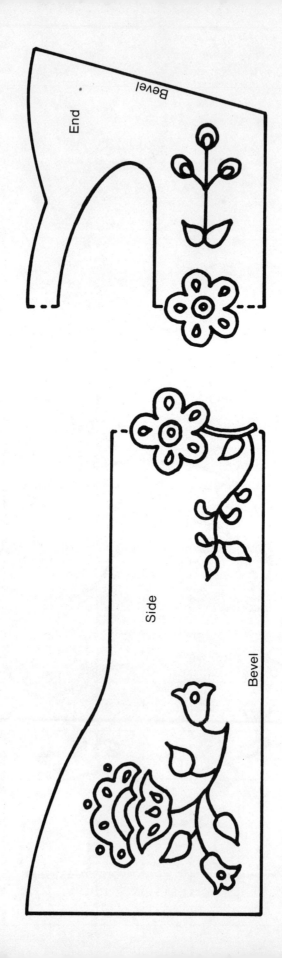

BREAD TRAY

Example of box, made from ¼″ plywood, with sides beveled at corners and bottom.

Note: See color photo on page 3 of insert.

CRAYON AND CHALK HOLDER

Cut ends per pattern (two sides 2″ × 6½″, and bottom 4½″ × 6½″) from ¼″ plywood. Crayon holder is a 6½″ piece of two-by-four (actual size 1¾″ × 3½″ × 6½″). Center pattern on two-by-four to locate ⅜″ holes for crayons. Set drill point at intersection of grid lines.

Note: See color photo on page 7 of insert.

Cut out

Cut two

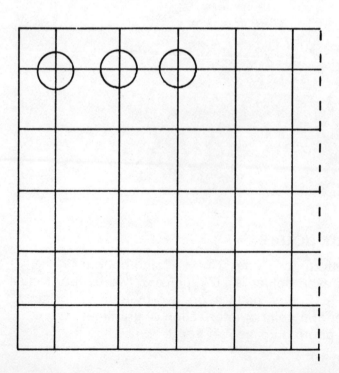

ONION BOX

This project uses a dowel hinge for the lift-up top. Front is cut out on jigsaw, but could also be made using dowels for front grille. Figures on back are applied pieces, but could also be painted directly on the back.

Use ¼" plywood, except for lid, which is ½" pine or basswood. Back is 8" × 12"; front, 5¼" × 7½"; bottom, 5¾" × 7½"; sides, 6" × 6"; lid, 5⅞" × 7½". Round back edge of lid by sanding, so it turns easily. Insert ³⁄₁₆" dowel through sides into lid (⅝" in from back of box) to serve as hinge. Glue dowel in sides but not in lid.

Note: See color photo on page 3 of insert.

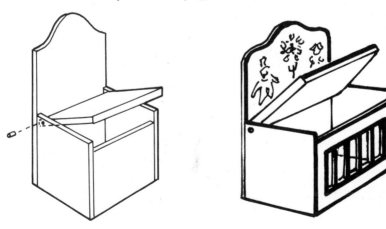

Top
of back

Continue pattern for 9"

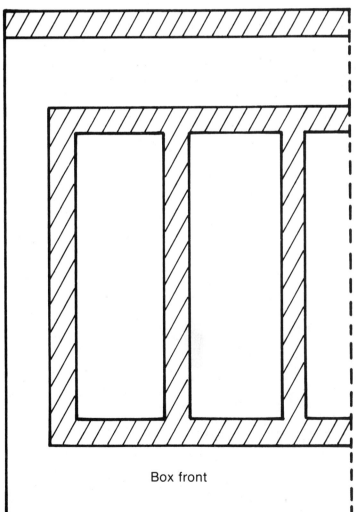

Box front

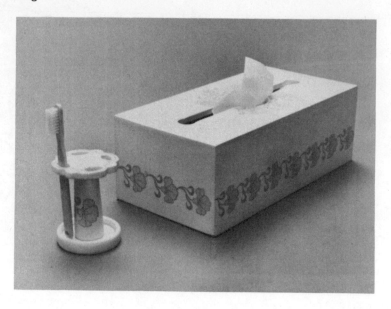

BATHROOM SET

Use ¼″ plywood. Tissue box requires one piece 5½″ × 10¾″ for top, two pieces 3½″ × 10¾″ for sides, and two pieces 3½″ × 5″ for ends. Complete half-pattern, center on top, and cut out.

To make bottom for tooth brush holder, cut two circles of plywood at once, and then cut out center of one for rim, as shown. Glue together and round edges of rim by sanding. Post is 1⅛″ dowel tapered by shaping on Moto-Shop sanding disk. Attach top and bottom to post with ¼″ dowel and glue.

Waste basket is ¼″ plywood. Cut four sides per pattern and bevel vertical edges at 45° angle. Cut base 6½″ × 6½″ and bevel edges at 7° angle. For ease of cleaning, cut an acrylic plastic liner to fit inside of wastebasket.

Note: See color photo on page 2 of insert.

8½″

Top opening

10½″

Top

Base

Rim

Bottom

Top

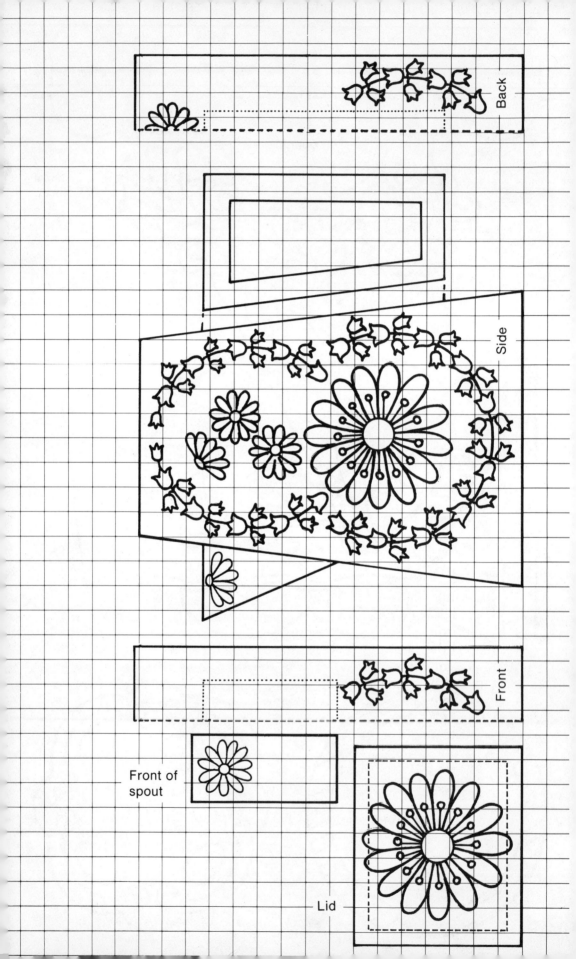

Back

Side

Front

Front of
spout

Lid

FLOWER HOLDER

Cut front, back, two sides, top, and bottom (3″ × 5½″, not shown) from ¼″ plywood. Cut inner top 3″ × 3½″ from ⅛″ plywood. Cut handle from 1″ solid stock. Knob is ⅝″ dowel, ⅝″ long. The front of spout and the back and front pieces of the container are longer to compensate for the diagonal shape of the sides. Assemble spout, and bevel top and base edges by sanding so they fit properly. Bevel edges of base to angle of sides. Assemble front, back, and sides around base, joining with glue and nails. Bevel top and base edges of front and back on Moto-Tool sanding wheel until they are level with sides. Glue spout to front piece, centering horizontally in position shown on pattern. Before assembling, attach handle to back piece with glue and nails. Center and glue inner top to top. Attach knob to top with screw.

Note: See color photo on page 2 of insert.

MINI-BOOKSHELF

Use ¼″ plywood to cut patterns and a 5″ × 5¾″ bottom. This project can be used two ways: In one position it's a mini-bookshelf; in the other it's a holder for pencils, phone memo book, and notepaper to hang or place near telephone.

Note: See color photo on page 3 of insert.

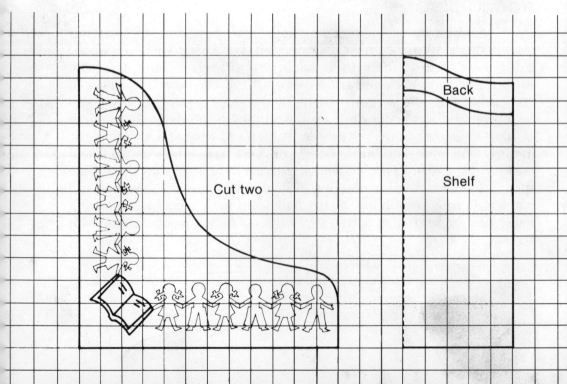

Cut two

Back

Shelf

CLOWN-SHAPED SORTER BOX

Materials:

Plywood ¼" (except sorter blocks which are 1" solid stock):
Sides—4¼" × 6" (cut two)
Back—4¼" × 5½"
Bottom—3¾" × 4¼"
Guides and trim for lid—¼" × 4¼" (cut five)

Join head to body for full-size pattern. Cut out and sand sorter blocks. Locate shapes on box as desired, being sure they are placed below guides for sliding lid. Trace around shapes and use as cutting pattern for openings. Assemble box as illustrated.

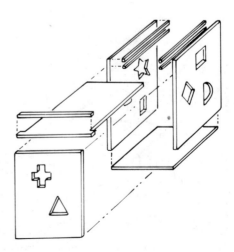

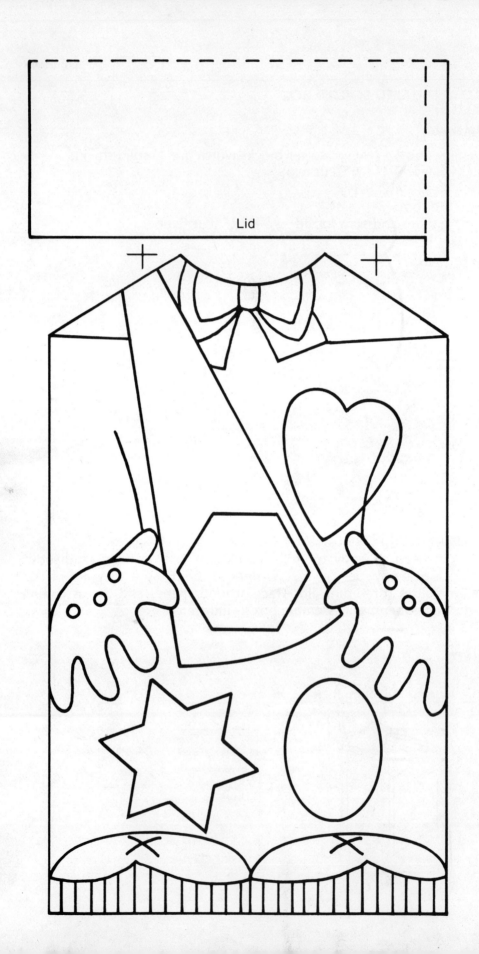
Lid

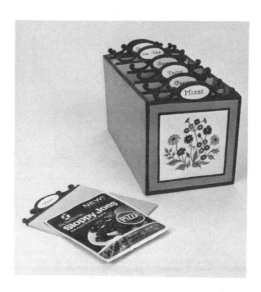

PREPARED-MIX BOX

A convenient storage box for prepared-mix envelopes. Label dividers to identify types you use. Size can be altered to make recipe holder, phone number and address file, etc. Box is ¼″ plywood; dividers, ⅛″ plywood. Pattern is for front and back of box. Trace on broken line for dividers. Sides are 5½″ × 10½″, inset bottom 5″ × 10½″.

Note: See color photo on page 3 of insert.

UTENSIL HOLDER

Use for purchased utensils, or make your own. Spaghetti server pictured is a flat spoon shape with ¼″ dowels inserted. Spoons are rough cut on saw and shaped with Moto-Tool. Holder is a box of ¼″ plywood with an elevated back. Back is 4″ × 10½″; sides, 2¾″ × 5½″; front, 4″ × 5½″; top and bottom, 2¾″ × 3½″. Cut and drill openings in top, per pattern. Glue top, bottom, and sides in place before adding front. Reduced patterns show details for painting. Do them freehand or enlarge and trace pattern on gessoed wood.

Note: See color photo on page 3 of insert.

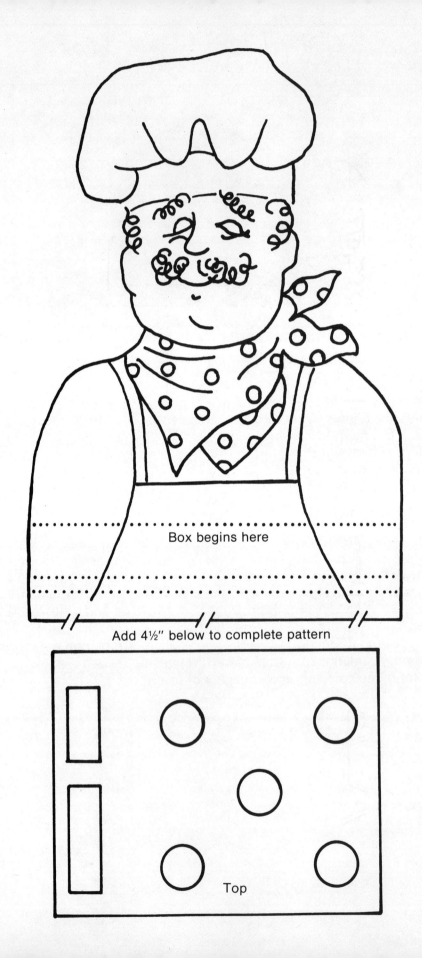

Box begins here

Add 4½" below to complete pattern

Top

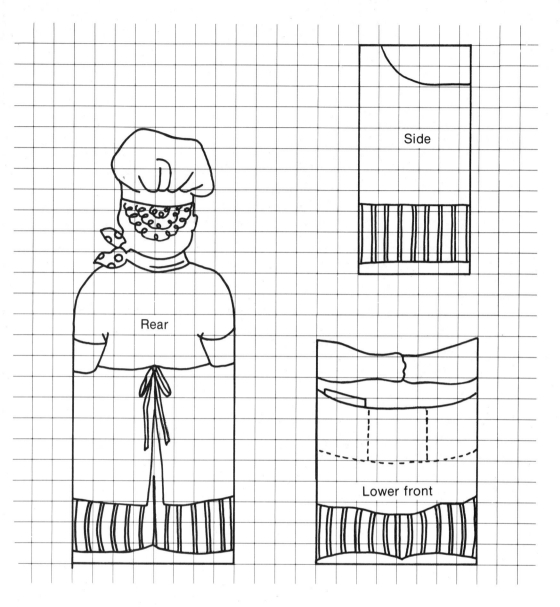

Side

Rear

Lower front

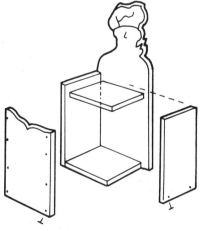

TEENAGE BEAUTY CENTER

Materials:

> Plywood ¼″:
>   Back—11½″ × 21½″
>   Front—5¾″ × 11½″
>   Ends—2″ × 5¾″ (cut two)
>   Dividers—2″ × 5½″ (cut two)
>   Bottom—2″ × 11″
> Mirror—5½″ × 10″
> Fabric trim—5′

This project combines wood with fabric and a mirror to create an appealing accessory for a young lady. Complete patterns as shown and cut all pieces. Assemble box. Complete painting, and glue mirror in place. Glue on trim as shown in illustration. Although designed to hang on the wall, it can also stand on a high dresser or bookcase.

Note: See color photo on page 3 of insert.

Front

15 Wood with other materials

SEWING CADDY

Materials:

Plywood ¼":
  Back—7" × 17"
  Front and bottom—1½" × 5¾"
  Sides—1½" × 3¾" (cut two)
  Shelf—1½" × 5¾"
Dowel—¼" × 1¾" (cut three)
Fabric, elastic, lace, foam rubber

Transfer patterns and cut all pieces. Make scissor and dowel holes in shelf. Insert dowels after painting. To make pincushion hat, cut 6" circle of fabric; sew on gathered lace ⅝" from edge. Fold edge under, and stitch to create casing for elastic drawstring. Glue foam rubber to upper portion of head, and put on hat.

Note: See color photo on page 2 of insert.

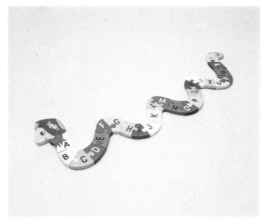

Alphabet worm (p. 44)

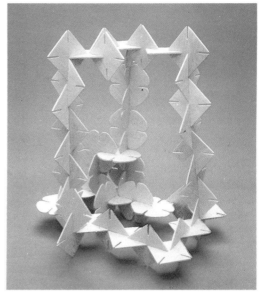

Diamonds and clover (p. 46)

Special occasion plaques (p. 55)
Teddy bear coatrack (enlarged
ornament from "Cookie-Cutter
Christmas Tree," p. 59)

Cat memo board (enlarged ornament from
"Cookie-Cutter Christmas Tree," p. 59)

Cookie-cutter Christmas tree (p. 59)

Thanksgiving plaque (p. 85)

Containers (p. 90), Kangaroo box (p. 97), Butterfly and snowman box (p. 93)

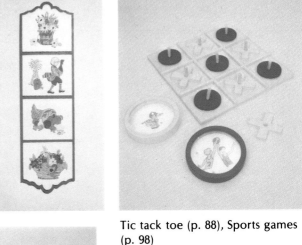

Tic tack toe (p. 88), Sports games (p. 98)

Bathroom set (p. 108)

Flower holder (p. 112)

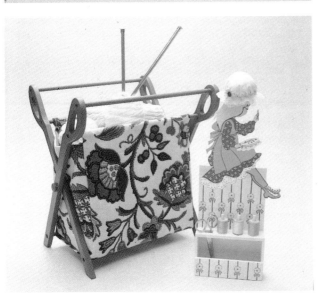

Knitting bag (p. 125), Sewing caddy (p. 122)

Prepared-mix box (p. 117)

Mini-bookshelf (p. 112), Piggy bank (p. 100), Race car (p. 83)

Macrame and tile planter (p. 129)

Teenage beauty center (p. 120)

Onion box (p. 105), Bread tray (p. 103)

Utensil holder (p. 117), Egg holder or trivet (p. 97), Clown cup and dish holders (p. 53)

Hanging plant or curio shelf (p. 129), Purse handles (p. 127)

Pet dish holder (p. 150)

Above left—Nativity scene (p. 132)

Above center—One-piece candelabra (p. 145)

Above right—Decoupage (p.142)

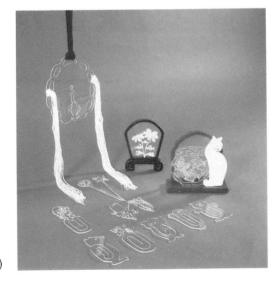

Fun with plastic (p. 135)

Rocking horse (p. 155)

Doll house furniture (p. 157)

Cosmetic case (p. 166)

Paint holder (p. 165)

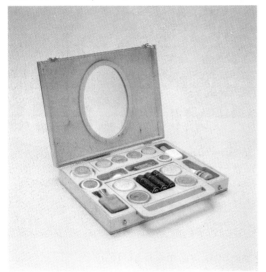

Below left—Baby toys and rattles (p. 152)
Dog pull toy (p. 83)

Below right—Puzzles: Crooked man (p. 147),
Container (p. 90), Doghouse (p. 48),
Silhouette (p. 78)

Portable chess set (p. 187)

Three bears pull toy (178)

Mug holder (p. 175)

Christmas ornaments (p. 161)

Tiger tape holder (p. 168)

Garden shadow box (p. 198)

Kangaroo chair (p. 188)

Noah's ark mobile (p. 182)

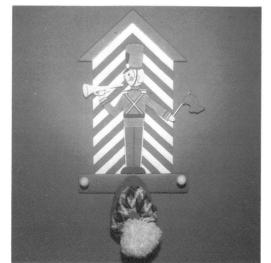

Soldier coat rack (p. 192)

Elephant tea cart (p. 190)

Stay-in-bed tray (p. 206), Crayon and chalk holder
(p. 103)
Christmas card holder (p. 203)

Chess book (p. 235) Iron caddy (p. 237) Cat chow box (p. 217)

Heron (p. 241), Gulls (p. 239)

Above right—Gingerbread house
(p. 210)

Owl (p. 243), Urn (p. 241)

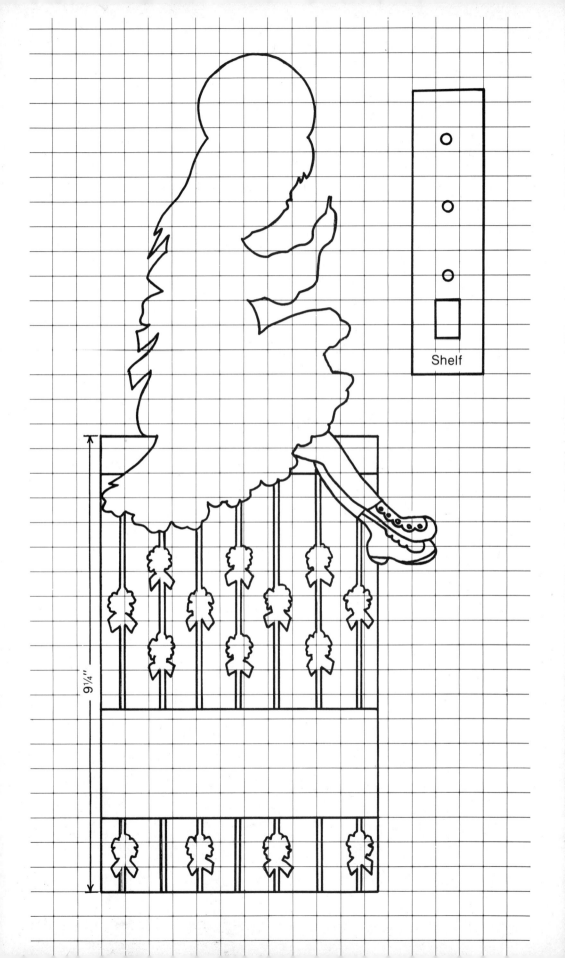

Shelf

9¼"

Painting detail

Macrame by Michelle Muller

KNITTING BAG

Materials:

Plywood ½"—12" × 14" (for scissor blades)
Dowels ⅜"—six pieces 13", two pieces 1"
Fabric or macrame

Join scissor blades with 13" dowels, as shown in diagram, making certain that handles are facing in correct direction. Join the two units with 1" dowel pieces, gluing them into outer blades only. Bag may be made of fabric or macrame.

Note: See color photo on page 2 of insert.

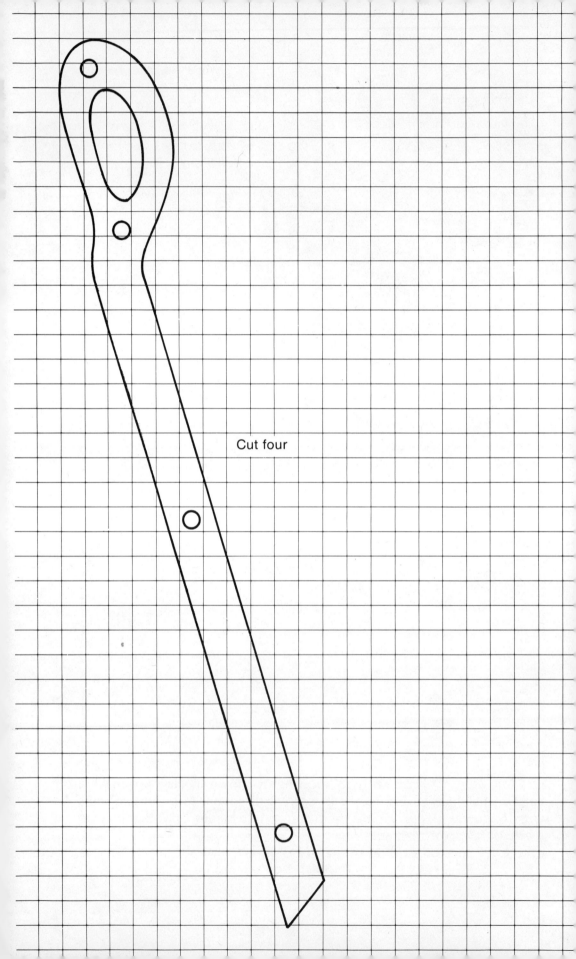

Cut four

PURSE HANDLES

Make your own purse handles and add your choice of macrame pattern or fabric. Complete pattern and cut from ½" pine, basswood, or plywood, or even acrylic plastic sheets. Finish with wood stain of your choice and clear wood sealer, or paint and decorate. Size of handle can be adjusted to suit your needs.

Note: See color photo on page 4 of insert.

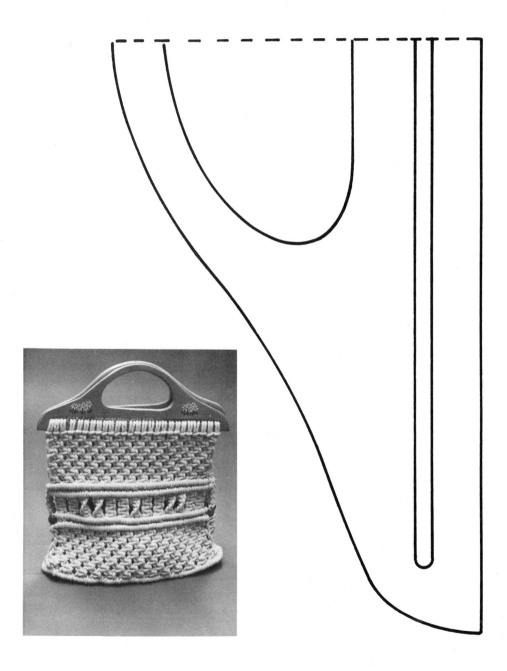

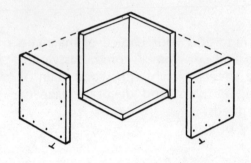

Wraparound butt joint

Detail for base of box

Macrame by Michelle Muller

MACRAME AND TILE PLANTER

Materials:

Plywood ¼″:
  Sides—6″ × 6¾″ (cut four)
  Bottom—5¾″ × 5¾″
  Tiles—¼″

Macrame enthusiasts can make many accessories from wood to enhance the beauty of their work. Here, plywood is painted to resemble Delft tile and is glued to the sides of a hanging planter box. Box could also be hung from chain.

Trace base pattern detail on each side piece and cut. Drill ⁵⁄₃₂″ holes in upper corners for macrame ½″ from left side and ¼″ from right (short) side. Assemble box with wraparound butt joints, butting the short pattern end of one piece into long pattern side of next piece. Glue and nail bottom to sides ½″ above base pattern. Painted tiles are centered 1″ from top.

Note: See color photo on page 3 of insert.

HANGING PLANT OR CURIO SHELF

Cut and drill parts as shown, using ⅜″ plywood. Cut ⅜″ × ½″ slots in shelf carefully, to ensure tight fit. Create macrame hanger to suit your tastes, or use chain. Shelf may be glued in place, or remain loose for ease of storage.

Note: See color photo on page 4 of insert.

Macrame by Michelle Muller

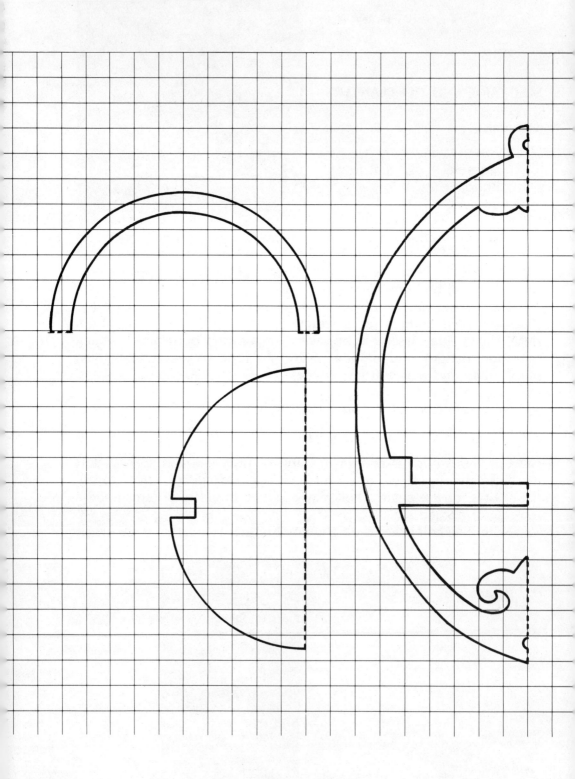

Macrame by Michelle Muller

NATIVITY SCENE

This is an exciting project for macrame enthusiasts, but the nativity figures can also be placed on a mantel, or the shelves may be suspended from silk braid or chain.

Shelves are ¼″ plywood circles, with diameters, 7½″, 9½″, and 11½″, spaced vertically so that the macrame hanger forms the shape of a Christmas tree. Figures are ⅜″ plywood, except grass under stable, which is ⅛″. Drill four, evenly spaced 5/32″ holes in each shelf for macrame. Drill holes in star halves and angels before cutting them out. Star pieces cross lap. Use Christmas ornament hooks to make crooks for shepherds.

Note: See color photo on page 4 of insert.

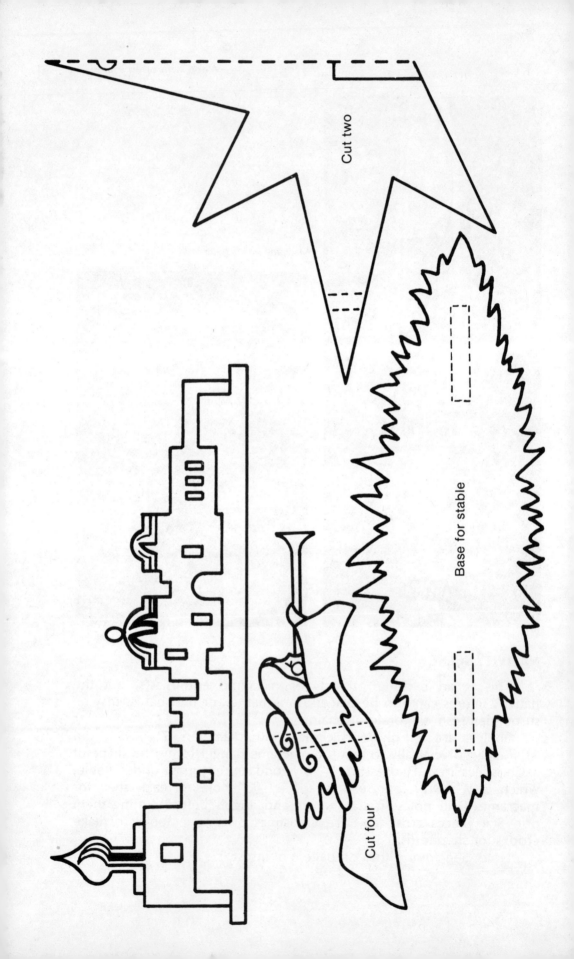

Cut two

Base for stable

Cut four

FUN WITH PLASTIC

Wood can be combined with plastic in a variety of ways to increase the usefulness of your creations or add interest to them. Some items in this book—for example, the wastebasket and the drawers in the paint holder—will be more serviceable if you construct acrylic liners for them. Acrylic can also be substituted for glass in picture frames or cut and etched to enhance decorative pieces, such as the fish bowl for the napkin holder that is included in this section.

Acrylic plastic sheets—marked in various thicknesses and colors under brand names such as Lexan, Plexiglas, and Lucite—cut easily on the Moto-Shop.

Patterns should be traced on the protective sheet with which the plastic is covered. Don't try to transfer the pattern by tracing over carbon paper. Instead, lay the clear plastic sheet over the pattern and trace directly on the protective cover with a magic marker pen. While working with the acrylic, leave the protective cover on to prevent scratching and fusing.

Work should be fed slowly to prevent the acrylic from getting so

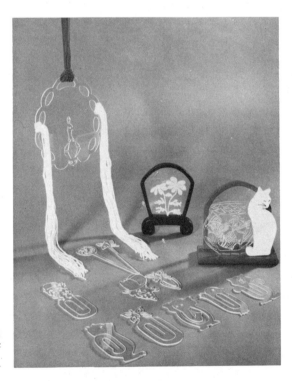

See "Oriental Flower" and "Napkin Holder" for patterns of two of the objects pictured here.

hot that the kerf fuses behind the blade. Edges can be smoothed with medium grit, aluminum oxide paper. If a smoother finish is desired, sand further with fine grit (#200) wet-or-dry paper. A transparent

glossy finish can be restored to the edges by sanding with #400 or #500 paper and buffing on a wheel with a special compound made for this purpose. Be careful not to overheat the acrylic while buffing.

Holes can be drilled in acrylic with the drill on the Moto-Shop flexible shaft, or with any standard twist drill. Drill all of the holes that a pattern requires before beginning to saw; plastic is fragile, so predrilling helps prevent breakage. Acrylic can be glued with specially designed products that are available where the sheets are sold. The processes differ depending upon the type of glue used, so read directions carefully.

You can have a lot of fun making novelty items from plastic scraps. Fascinating designs can be created simply by drilling an entry hole and using the jigsaw blade to cut the detail. The kerf turns white, establishing a visible pattern in the acrylic sheet.

A few ideas for novelty items are pictured. They include large paper clips, swizzle sticks designed to suit an occasion, and a peacock to keep your needlepoint yarn sorted and tangle-free. Try making some of these, and then use your imagination to design your own scrap art.

Note: See color photo on page 4 of insert.

ORIENTAL FLOWER

Inspired by oriental cork carvings, this attractive, decorative item can be used also as a two-way picture frame. Outside frames and flower are $\frac{1}{8}$" plywood; center section of frame, $\frac{3}{8}$" plywood, with opening $\frac{1}{4}$" larger to accommodate two pieces of $\frac{1}{8}$" acrylic; base, 1" pine. Cut slot in base of center section and insert flower stem, using glue. Drill dowel holes and assemble parts, as illustrated.

Note: See photo of "Oriental Flower" under "Fun With Plastic"; also see color photo on page 4 of insert.

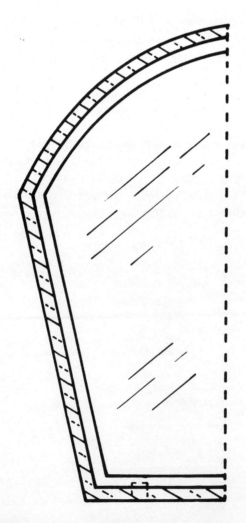

NAPKIN HOLDER

This novel combination of wood and plastic can be used as a napkin or letter holder.

Frame: Nail three pieces of ⅛″ plywood together; trace pattern on top and cut around outlines. Sand edges before removing nails. In two ⅛″ outer pieces, make openings by cutting along solid lines. Make opening in center piece by cutting along broken line. Cut acrylic to fit opening in center piece. Insert plastic and glue pieces together. Drill two ⅛″ dowel holes in bottom of frame to attach it to base.

Cat: Nail three pieces of ⅛″ plywood together; trace pattern and cut around outline. Sand edges and remove nails. Cut center piece on broken line and glue cat pieces together. Drill ⅛″ dowel holes to attach cat to base.

Base: Complete half pattern and transfer to 1″ pine board, 2½″ × 6½″. Drill dowel holes with ⅛″ drill. Cut slots with knife or #107 cutter on Moto-Tool.

Fish Bowl: Place ⅛″ acrylic over pattern and trace it on protective covering with magic marker pen. Don't trace pattern for etched design. After sawing, remove protective sheet; lay fish bowl over pattern, and etch the design with Moto-Tool engraving cutters or a fine-pointed instrument.

Glue cat and frame in place, using ⅛″ dowel. Slide fish bowl into opening in cat and insert base projections into slots in base.

Note: See photo of "Napkin Holder" under "Fun With Plastic"; also see color photo on page 4 of insert.

Base

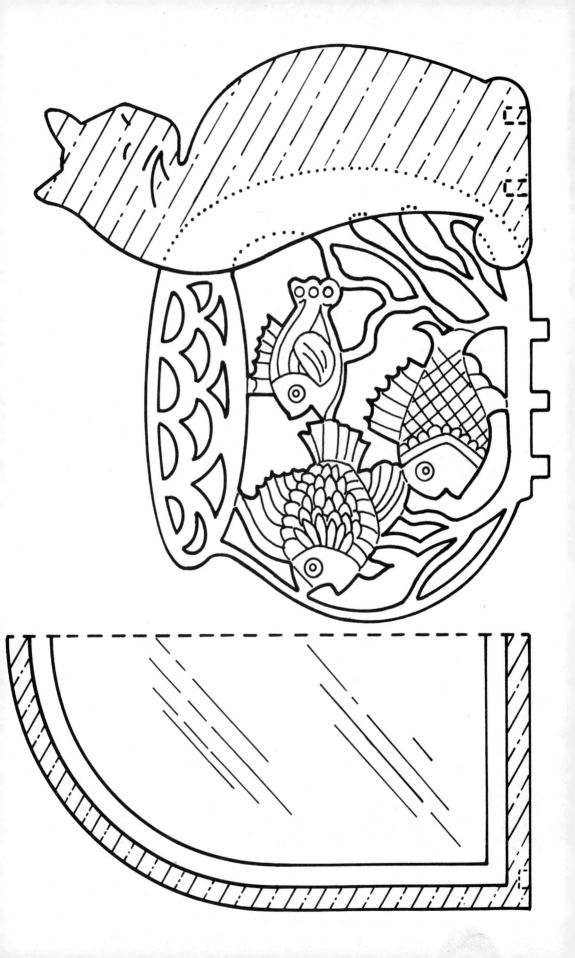

DECOUPAGE

Decoupage fanciers can broaden their horizons by using the jigsaw to get away from the standard plaques and boxes available in the hobby stores. The Moto-Tool and router can be used to shape the edges. Greeting cards, wallpaper, vinyl, contact paper, gift wrapping paper, seals, press-on letters, and other printed designs can be glued to wood and cut out, using the design as the cutting pattern. The piece is then finished by covering with Modge-Podge, as shown.

Using this technique as an alternative to painting, you can make most of the items described in this book in a relatively short time.

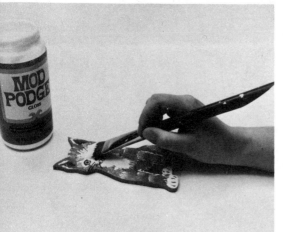

Follow the usual guidelines for decoupage

Standup toys

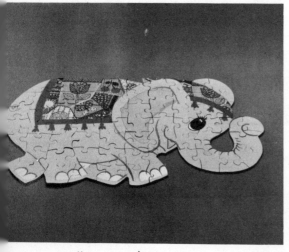

Jigsaw puzzle

Merry cutouts for children's rooms

Follow the usual guidelines for decoupage, but remember these pointers:

• When cutting paper that is glued to wood, keep the paper on top; paper glued to the bottom will fray.

• If you want duplicate pictures on both sides of a piece, cut around the design on one side first, and then glue the design to the other side and trim the edges with a sharp knife or razor blade.

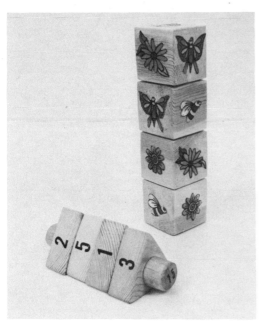

Simple games

Triptych

• If desired, sand the edges carefully, brushing the paper lightly to form a narrow, white, finish line around the item.

Pictured here are standup toys to illustrate how one could make the macrame nativity set using cutouts from Christmas cards. A special Christmas gift would be an unusual box made from a greeting card; the box could contain a music box or some other treasure. The attractive triptych was also made from greeting cards. Other items include puzzles, a decoupage version of a bedroom door plaque, and a whimsical clown that could be used as a switchplate cover. The plaque and the clown were made from wallpaper. Decoupage also offers a quick and easy way to make advertising displays for a puppet show, a children's musical, a theatrical event, or a garage sale.

For a very special birthday party, make a set like the one pictured here. Use your choice of gift-wrap paper, or cutouts from the party cups and plates you plan to use. Set the tone for the party by decoupaging one of the invitations to the front and back of a plywood

Box using Christmas card as cutting
pattern for top and bottom (right)

Cutout plaques (below)

Birthday party set

plaque, preserving it for the birthday child as a memento of the happy
day. Make individual name tags for the guests, using your chosen
design and press-on letters. Attach a brooch pin to the back with lots
of glue.

Make individual candy boxes by gluing design on the front piece
and cutting the silhouette outline at the top, leaving the square,
bottom half as the front of a simple butt joint box. Cake stand is
simply a round box with scalloped top and bottom.

Make some small gifts for the party guests and place them in the
box: toy animals or jewelry, perhaps. Set birthday cake on top of box
and distribute gifts after cake has disappeared. Gifts for the birthday
child may include oval plaques, if she's a ballet enthusiast, or a vinyl
placemat made into a wooden puzzle.

Note: See color photo on page 4 of insert.

16 Advanced projects

ONE-PIECE CANDELABRA

Materials:

Basswood $\frac{1}{2}$"—9" × 10"
Dowel $\frac{1}{4}$"—7$\frac{1}{2}$"

Complete half pattern and transfer to wood. Mark center line lightly, as guide for drilling dowel holes. After cutting out branches, remove "cap" piece. Mark center point on top of remaining pieces and use drill guide to drill $\frac{1}{4}$" hole through them. With Moto-Tool or pointed knife, make recess in cap to cover end of center dowel. Sand and shape cap so it will not extend over branch below. Slightly enlarge holes in all pieces except cap and base, using sandpaper or rasp, so that they will turn freely but not loosely on the dowel.

Carefully sand all sides and round off all edges of branches to be sure they don't bind when turned. Using drill or Moto-Tool, make candle holes in top end of each branch. Gesso and paint all pieces separately. Glue cap to dowel and thread on remaining pieces. Before gluing dowel in base, check to make sure branches turn freely, and cut off any excess dowel.

Note: See color photo on page 4 of insert.

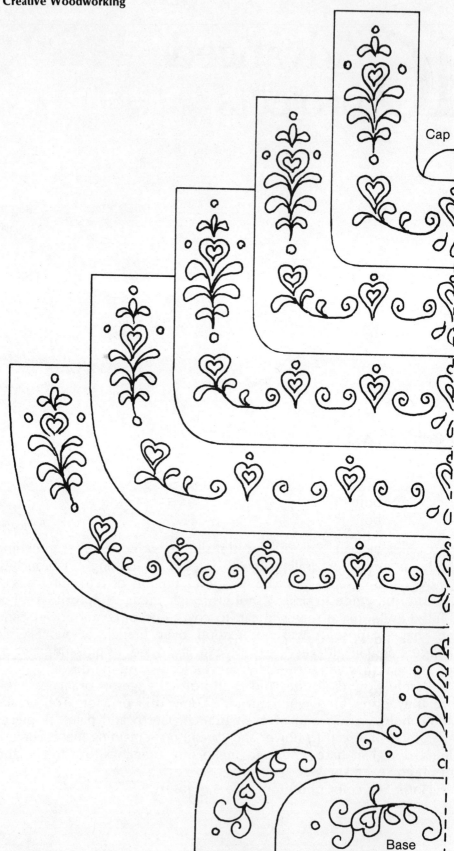

Cap

Base

CROOKED MAN PUZZLE

Materials:

> Top and bottom—$\frac{1}{2}$" basswood, 2" × 7"
> Top and bottom of door—$\frac{3}{4}$" basswood, $\frac{3}{4}$" × 7"
> Door—$\frac{1}{8}$" birch plywood, 6" × 10"
> Puzzle—$\frac{5}{8}$" basswood
> Sides—$\frac{1}{4}$" dowels, $12\frac{1}{2}$" long (cut fifteen)

Cut parts and drill dowel holes as shown. Rout grooves $\frac{1}{8}$" deep in top and bottom of door to receive plywood piece. Make sure parts are positioned as shown in photo before cutting grooves with Moto-Tool or chisel. Assemble project and glue dowel in place. Cut crooked-man-puzzle pieces on heavy lines only. Light lines are painting pattern; to avoid confusion during cutting, trace over them in a different color.

Note: See color photo on page 5 of insert.

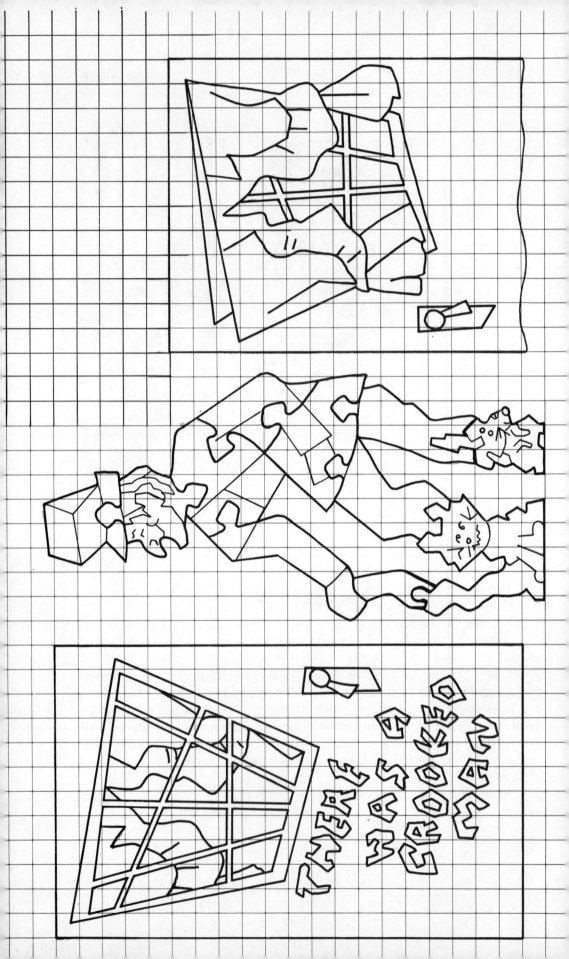

THERE WAS A CROOKED MAN

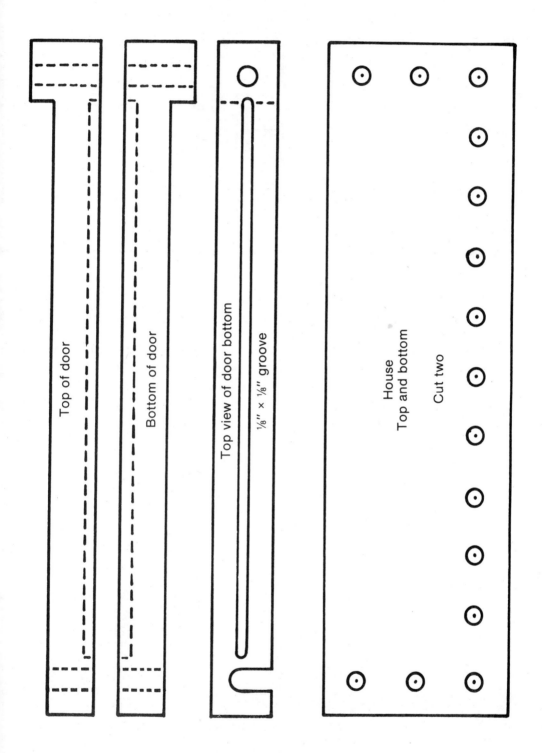

Top of door

Bottom of door

Top view of door bottom

⅛" × ⅛" groove

House
Top and bottom

Cut two

PET DISH HOLDER

Keep your cat's dish out of sight behind this attractive holder. Cut cat figure from ¼" plywood. Nail two 6" × 6" pieces of ½" plywood together, placing nails near center of pieces. Trace dish holder pattern on top piece and cut both pieces simultaneously, on outer outline only. Drill seven ¼" dowel holes where indicated, going through both pieces. Separate pieces and cut center opening in top piece. Assemble unit using ¼" × 2" dowels. Fasten unit to back of cat, using nails or screws, and glue.

Variations of the pet dish holder:
• If your pet is canine, substitute a dog figure taken from a coloring book or other source.
• Substitute a wedge for the dish holder to make a door stop.
• If you don't have a pet, use dish holder as a plant holder.
Note: See color photo on page 4 of insert.

BABY TOYS AND RATTLES

To make action baby-toys, which have moving parts, cut from ¾" basswood. Drill dowel holes before cutting out pieces. Sand outer ends of ¼" dowels so revolving parts will turn freely. Glue figures to dowels. Cut dowels slightly short and fill outer ends of dowel holes with wood filler so that dowels will remain in place.

Note: See color photo on page 5 of insert. (Simple toys made from cookie-cutter patterns are shown in addition to the action baby toys.)

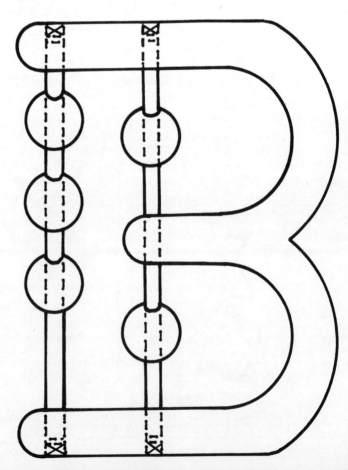

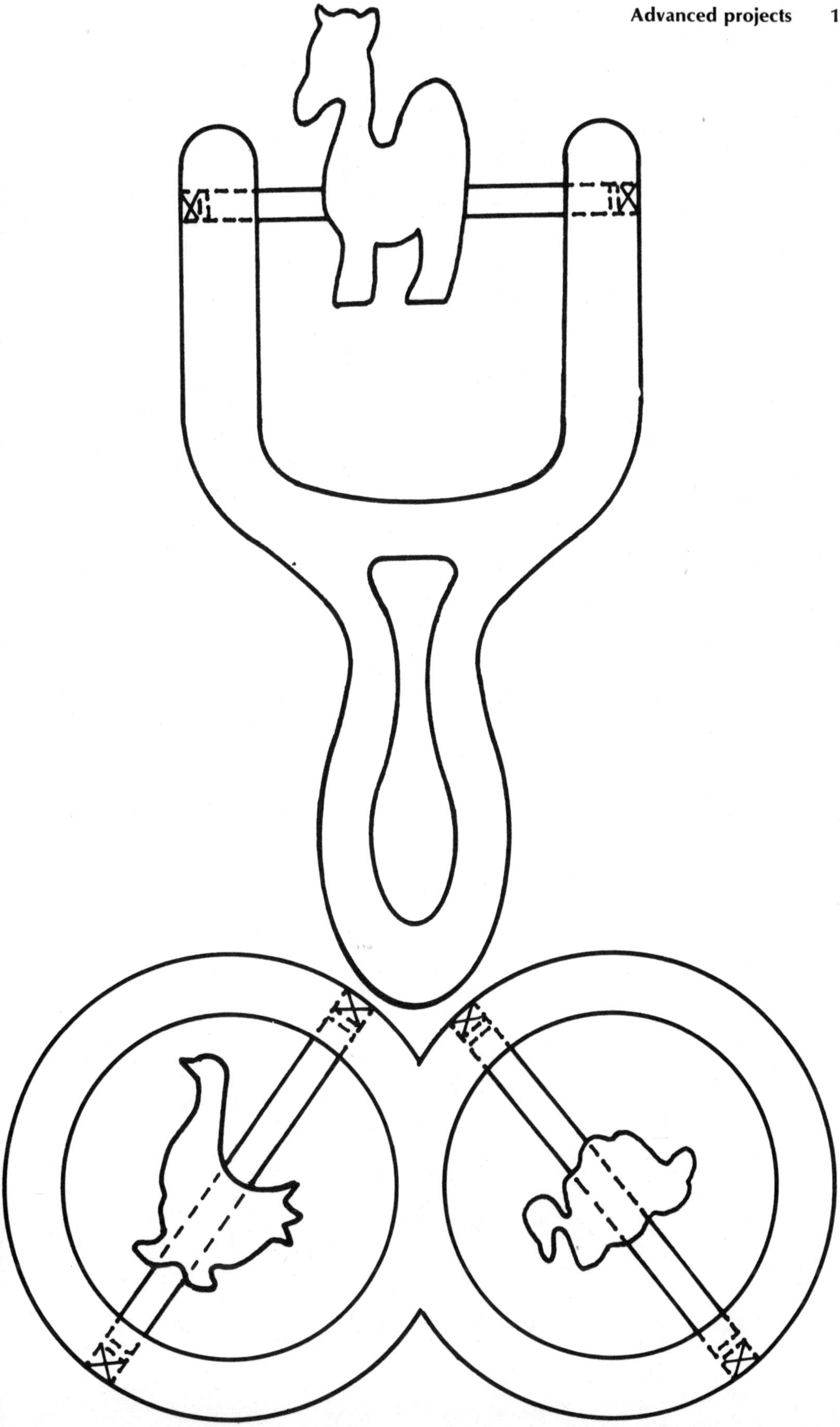

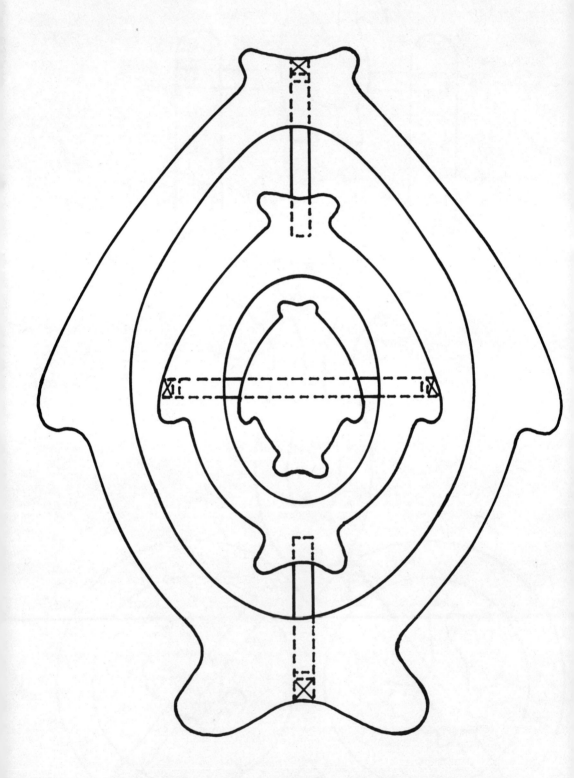

ROCKING HORSE

This is a simple project to cut and paint, but extreme care must be taken in assembly. Some trial and error will be required in locating the dowel holes that attach the legs to the seat: The chosen placement must balance the horse.

The parts, if traced carefully, can be cut from a 5½' length of clear pine one-by-twelve. Miter tops of the legs at 19° and seat back at 10°, as shown on pattern. Drill ¼" dowel holes. Use dowel kit to locate dowel holes in rockers, exercising care to maintain the proper angles. Assemble legs and rockers. Drill 1" hole in head for 1" × 6" dowel

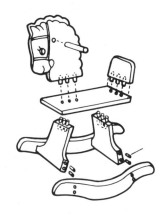

handle. Assemble seat, head with handle, and seat back, as shown in diagram. Insert dowel markers in holes on tops of legs, and set seat on top. Center it and adjust forward or backward until balance is achieved. Mark dowel locations by pressing seat against markers, and drill holes ½" deep, following angle of dowels. Paint parts separately and reassemble, gluing dowels in place.

Hint: Drilling errors can be corrected by gluing dowel into hole, flush with surface, and redrilling.

Note: See color photo on page 5 of insert.

Miter 19°

Miter 10°

Miter angle—
seat back

Miter angle—
legs

DOLL HOUSE FURNITURE

These examples of miniature furniture were made from ⅛″ plywood unless otherwise indicated. You can design your own by reducing the scale of furniture in your house. Parts can be shaped and rounded, and detail added, by using sandpaper and small files. Toothpicks or small dowels can also be substituted for some parts.

Assemble parts with glue, but be careful not to get any on surfaces or they won't stain properly. Fabric can be glued on, where required, to simulate seat cushions. Applied pieces can be added to provide detail, as is done on the headboard and footboard of the bed. Dining room table top is 3″ × 6″. Picnic table top is 2″ × 3¾″. Bed bottom is 2″ × 3″. Use ⅛″ × 3″ dowel for park bench. Paint it, and picnic table, green.

Note: See color photo on page 5 of insert.

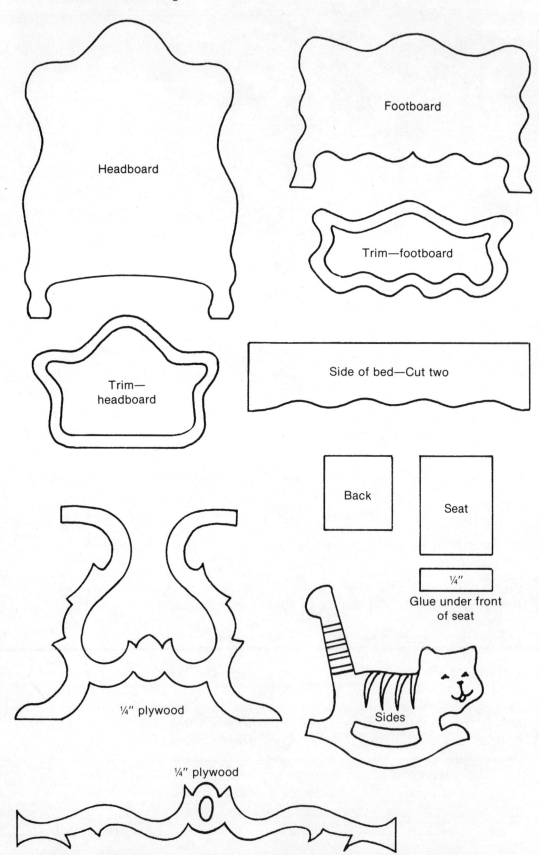

Headboard

Footboard

Trim—footboard

Trim—headboard

Side of bed—Cut two

Back

Seat

¼"

Glue under front
of seat

¼" plywood

Sides

¼" plywood

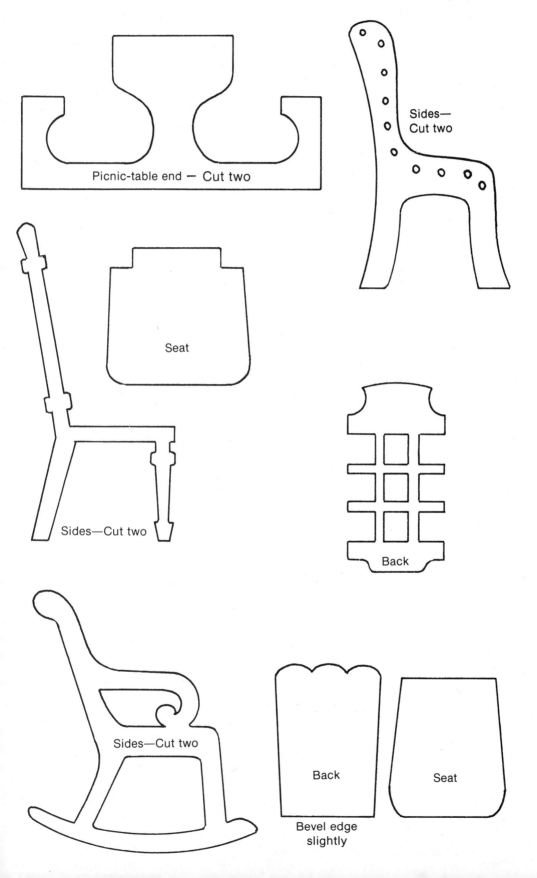

Picnic-table end — Cut two

Sides—
Cut two

Seat

Sides—Cut two

Back

Sides—Cut two

Back

Bevel edge
slightly

Seat

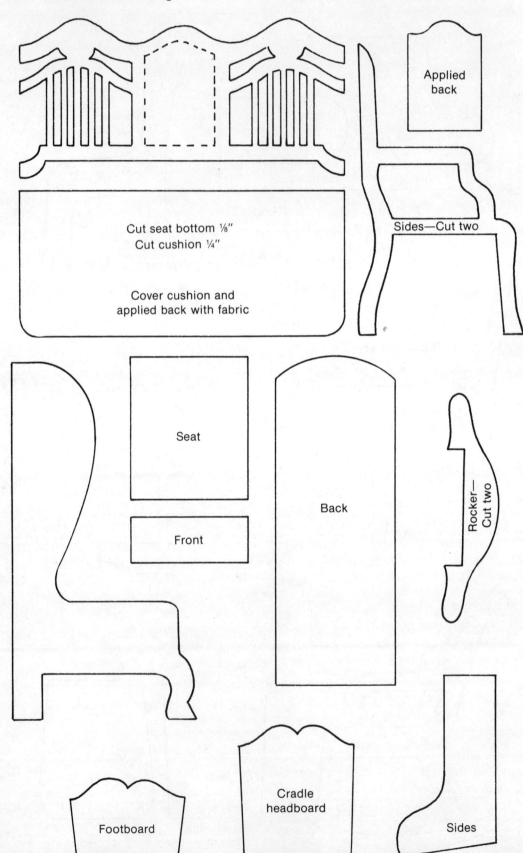

Cut seat bottom ⅛"
Cut cushion ¼"

Cover cushion and
applied back with fabric

Applied
back

Sides—Cut two

Seat

Front

Back

Rocker—
Cut two

Footboard

Cradle
headboard

Sides

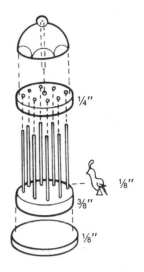

CHRISTMAS ORNAMENTS

Materials:

Plywood—⅛″, ¼″, and ⅜″
Pine—1″ × 2″
Dowel—⅛″
Acetate sheet, wood beads, string
(Above materials may be gathered from scraps.)

Santa: Cut two from ⅛″ material. Cut acetate and photo to insert behind opening. Glue pieces together. Drill tiny hole for string.

Hobby Horse: Head, ¼″ plywood. Dowel, ⅛″ × 3½″, small wooden bead.

Bird in Cage: For top use 1½″ wooden bead that has been cut in half as illustrated. Join pieces and small wooden bead with ⅛″ × 1¼″ dowel. Use eight pieces ⅛″ × 2″ dowel for cage, and assemble as illustrated.

Primitive Bird: Body is ½″ solid stock, wings and tail ⅛″. Use Moto-Tool or Exacto knife to shape neck, and drum sander or small wood file to round off body and head.

Train: Front, back, and sides—⅛″ plywood. Dowel (sanded flat on one side)—⅜″ × 1¼″. Pine for center roof (beveled as shown)—½″ × 1″ × 2″. Pine—1″ × 1″ × 1″. See assembly sketch.

Rocking Horse and Christmas Tree: Scaled down from other patterns in book.

Note: See color photo on page 6 of insert.

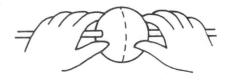

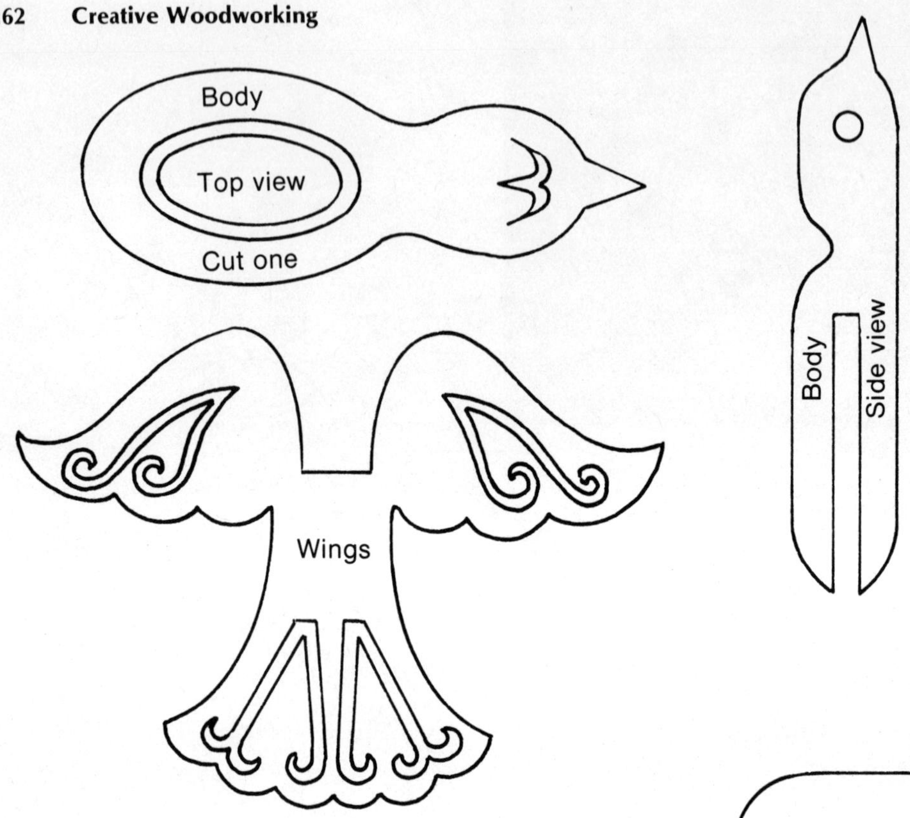

Body

Top view

Cut one

Body

Side view

Wings

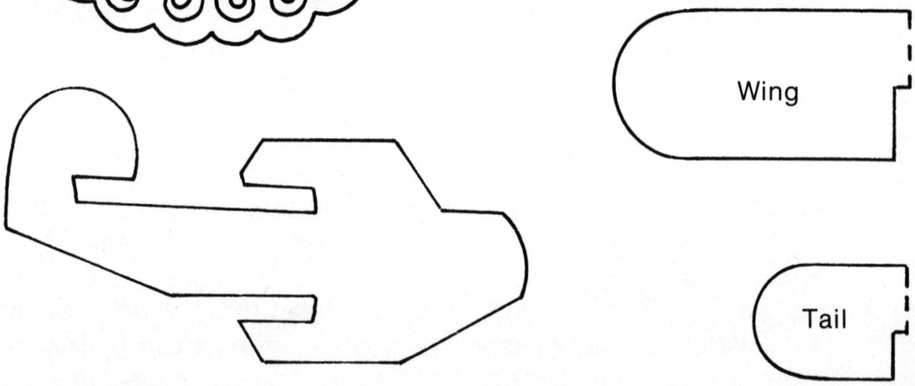

Wing

Tail

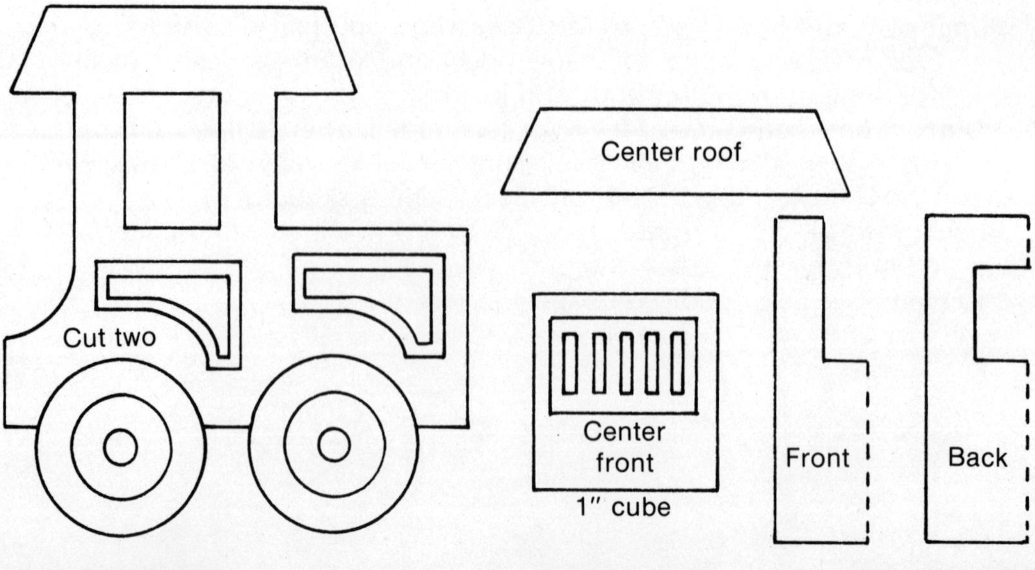

Center roof

Cut two

Center
front

1" cube

Front

Back

Painting

detail only

Cut two

Cage top
and base
pieces

Legs
—Cut two

Body

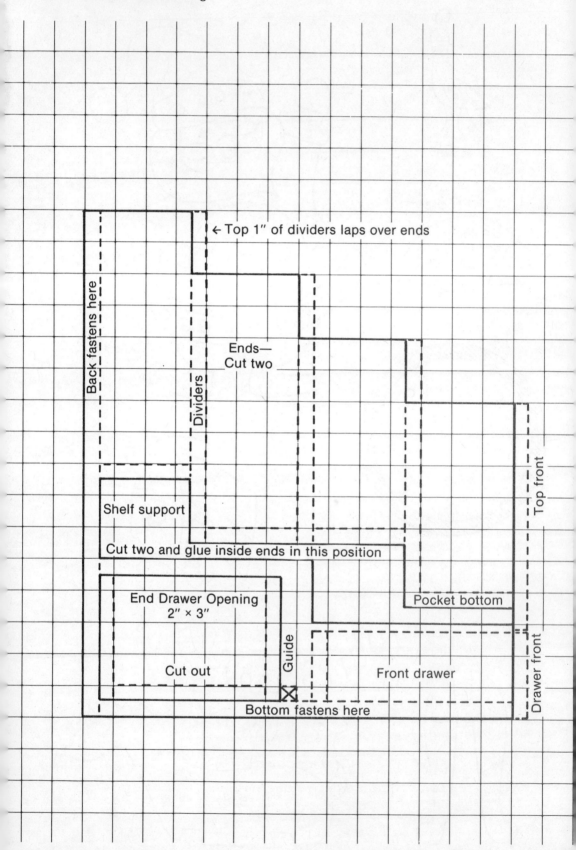

← Top 1" of dividers laps over ends

Back fastens here

Ends—
Cut two

Dividers

Shelf support

Cut two and glue inside ends in this position

End Drawer Opening
2" × 3"

Top front

Pocket bottom

Guide

Cut out

Front drawer

Drawer front

Bottom fastens here

PAINT HOLDER

Materials:

Plywood ¼" (2' × 5'):
  Back—8" × 23½"
  Top front—3⁹⁄₁₆" × 24"
  Horizontal dividers—5¼" × 24" (cut one)
                    —4¼" × 24" (cut two)
  Paint pocket bottoms—1½" × 23½" (cut four)
  Bottom—6¾" × 23½"
  Shelf support—(see patterns)
  Back drawer sides—2" × 23½" (cut two)
              bottom—2½" × 23½"
              ends—2" × 3" (cut two)
              guide—¼" × 23½"
  Front drawer bottom—3" × 23"
              back—1⅛" × 23"
              front—1⅜" × 24"
              ends—1⅛" × 3¼" (cut two)
Plywood ⅛" (8" × 24"):
  Small dividers—1½" × 4" (cut sixteen)
              —1½" × 3" (cut twenty-four)
Acrylic sheet for drawer liners, if desired.

Here's a handy rack to keep your paint tubes neatly organized and visible. Back drawer can be used for brush storage and front drawer, with plastic liner, for mixing paint. Holder may be adapted to other uses, as well.

Enlarge pattern; cut out two end pieces on solid outer lines. Cut out back drawer openings on solid lines. Cut two shelf supports and glue to inside of ends in position shown. Cut remaining pieces. Cut ¼" notch at each end of horizontal dividers, 1" from top, so dividers will overlap sides. Assemble drawers with inset bottoms, as shown. Glue back and ends to bottom of holder.

Put back-drawer in place and glue guide strip to bottom next to it, leaving only enough space so that it moves freely. Begin at back of box, and glue shelf bottoms and horizontal dividers in place, as shown. Attach top front. Insert small dividers for paint tube pockets, spacing them to suit your needs. Determine size of pockets, spacing them to suit your needs. Determine size of pockets and use blocks as guides to hold pieces in correct vertical position while you glue them. Finish box with clear wood sealer, or paint as you desire.

Note: See color photo on page 5 of insert.

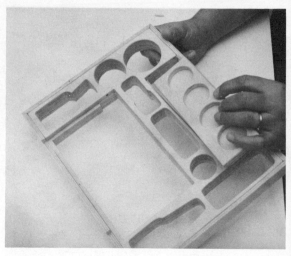

COSMETIC CASE

Materials:

Plywood—$\frac{1}{8}$" × 8" × 20"
—$\frac{1}{4}$" × 13" × 24"
—$\frac{3}{8}$" × 12" × 30"

At last, a place for everything: Cosmetics are neatly organized and easily accessible. Slim design makes this case ideal for home or travel use. Enlarge patterns and change opening shapes to fit your personal cosmetics. Transfer patterns to wood. Cut out all pieces and assemble, following photographs and assembly sketches. This case was made from Baltic Birch plywood, which is composed of alternating layers of light and dark veneer. When the sections were joined and sanded, the plywood created such an interesting design that the case was finished with a clear wood sealer only. However, it may be painted and personalized with a monogram. Small metal hinges and fasteners complete the project.

Note: See color photo on page 5 of insert.

Sides—$\frac{3}{4}$" × 11$\frac{1}{2}$" × $\frac{1}{4}$"
—$\frac{3}{4}$" × 9" × $\frac{1}{4}$"

Overlapped top—
9" × 11$\frac{1}{2}$" × $\frac{1}{4}$"

Center section—
10" × 11" × $\frac{3}{8}$"
Note: handle becomes lid for section below.

Bottom sections—
8$\frac{1}{2}$" × 11" × $\frac{3}{8}$"
(make two)

Sides—1" × 11$\frac{1}{2}$" × $\frac{1}{4}$"
—1" × 9" × $\frac{1}{4}$"

Overlapped bottom—
9" × 11$\frac{1}{2}$" × $\frac{1}{4}$"

5" × 7" oval mirror
$\frac{1}{8}$" frames

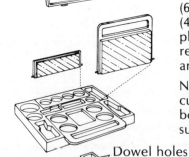

Dowel holes

Bottom of back lid ($6\frac{5}{8}$" × 2" × $\frac{1}{8}$") and front lid ($4\frac{1}{8}$" × $6\frac{3}{4}$" × $\frac{1}{8}$") are glued in place so that lids, when closed, rest on supports below. Lids are attached with $\frac{1}{8}$" dowels.

Note: compartment areas are cut $\frac{1}{8}$" smaller on the two bottom sections to form supports for lids.

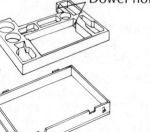

Glue center and bottom sections together. Sand all openings until smooth using drum sander on Moto-Tool or sandpaper wrapped around appropriate sized dowel.

Attach outside frame, hinges, and fasteners.

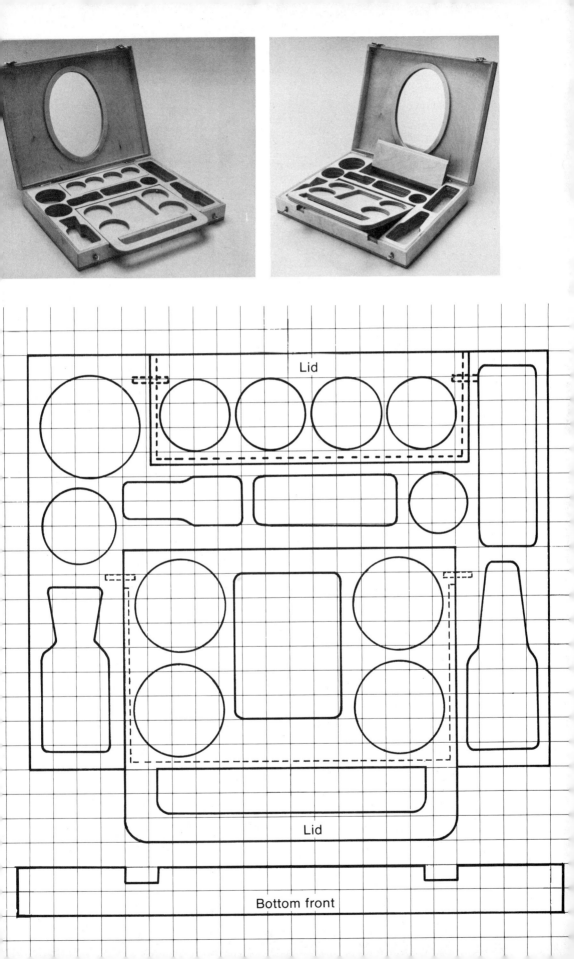

Lid

Lid

Bottom front

TIGER TAPE HOLDER

Materials:

    Upper Box—¼″ plywood (8″ × 24″):
      Sides—5½″ × 7¾″ (cut two)
      Top and Bottom—4¾″ × 5½″ (cut two)
      Back—4¼″ × 7¾″
    Lower Box—⅜″ plywood (12″ × 15″):
      Sides—4″ × 5¾″ (cut two)
      Divider—4″ × 5⅜″
      Top and Bottom—5½″ × 9½″ (cut two)
      Back—4″ × 8¾″
    Tiger—1″ pine (10″ × 2′, cut two)

This unit is designed to hold eight-track tapes, but box sizes can be altered to store albums or casettes.

Glue two tiger pieces together. Join tail to body with ¼″ dowel. Assemble boxes and attach tiger to lower one with ¼″ dowel and glue. Attach upper box with ¼″ dowel and glue.

Note: See color photo on page 6 of insert.

CRADLE GYM

Make one or all of the colorful, whimsical figures on this clever action toy. Cradle gym is easy to install, and pieces are interchangeable. Baby will enjoy watching it and learning to set the toys in motion. Child should not be left unattended with toy after he learns to sit up.

Cage: Expand support B; cut two and assemble as diagrammed. Cut two pieces of ½" pine from inner circle, cage pattern, drill blind dowel holes as indicated. Cut eight pieces of ¼" × 3½" dowel for cage and one piece of ¼" × 4" dowel for center. Insert several ¾" balls as cage is assembled. After painting, glue blocks together.

Bear: Assemble as diagrammed using two pieces of ¼" × 9" dowel. Bear is cut from ¾" pine, swing from ¼" plywood.

Clown: Expand support C and cut two. Cut clown from ¾" pine. Assemble with ¼" × 1½" dowel as diagrammed.

Spinning Wheel: Expand support A and cut two. Cut wheel from ¾" solid stock as indicated by pattern, and drill ⁵⁄₁₆" hole in center. Drill ⅜" holes in edge as shown. Cut six ⅜" × 3" dowels for spokes, and one ¼" × 1½" dowel for center support. Use ⅞" balls on ends of spokes.

Old Lady: Complete half-pattern. Cut arms, legs, and spacers for head and skirt from ½" solid stock. Drill ⅛" dowel holes in body and ³⁄₁₆" holes in arms. Insert ⅛" × ⅝" dowels in one outside piece and place arms over dowel. Install legs and assemble, gluing outside pieces to spacers only. Use ¼" × 4" dowel to suspend figure from block.

Boy/Girl End Supports: Cut figures from 2" × 4" × 5" pine. Heads are 1¾" wooden balls, attached with ¼" dowel. End cover is ⅛" × 1⅛" plywood circle, attached with a nail at top.

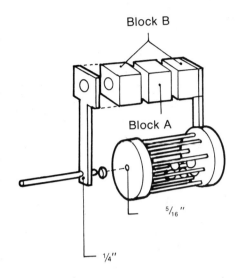

Block B

Block A

$^5/_{16}$ "

$^1/_4$ "

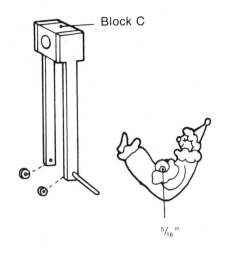

Block C

$^5/_{16}$ "

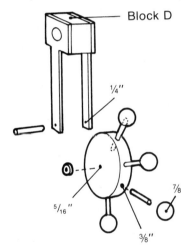

Block D

$^1/_4$ "

$^7/_8$

$^5/_{16}$ "

$^3/_8$ "

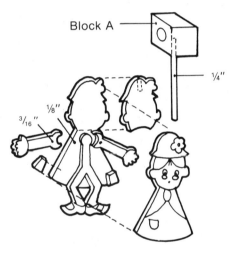

Block A

$^1/_4$ "

$^1/_8$ "

$^3/_{16}$ "

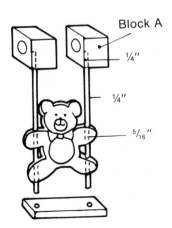

Block A

$^1/_4$ "

$^1/_4$ "

$^5/_{16}$ "

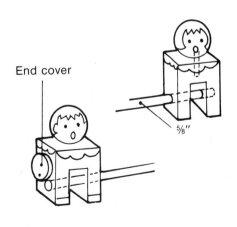

End cover

$^5/_8$ "

BLOCK CONSTRUCTION

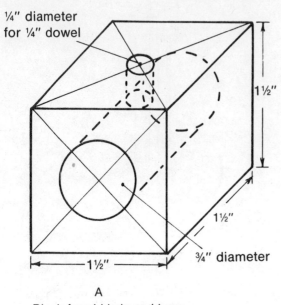

¼" diameter
for ¼" dowel

1½"

1½"

1½"

¾" diameter

A

Block for old lady and bear

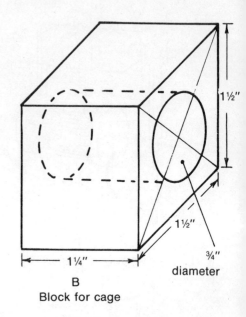

1½"

1½"

1¼"

¾"
diameter

B

Block for cage

Drill ¼" diameter hole as indicated

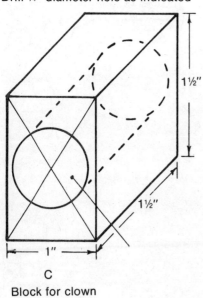

1½"

1½"

1"

C

Block for clown

1½"

1½"

1"

¾"
diameter

D

Block for spinning wheel

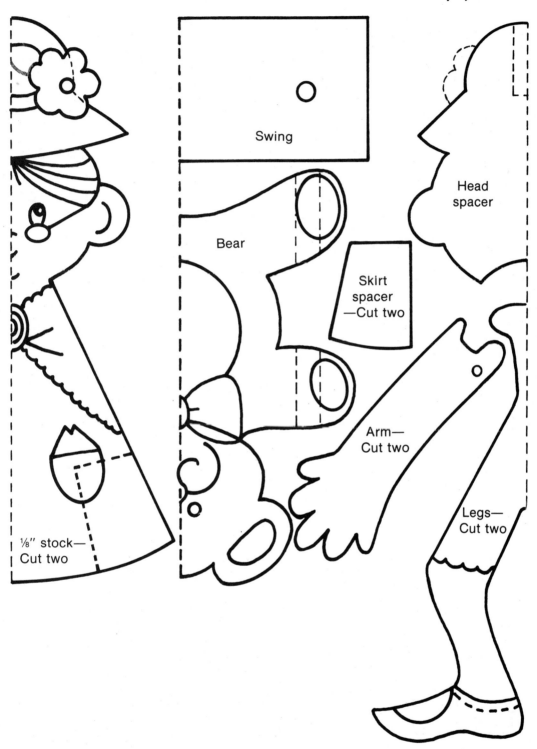

Swing

Bear

Head
spacer

Skirt
spacer
—Cut two

Arm—
Cut two

Legs—
Cut two

⅛″ stock—
Cut two

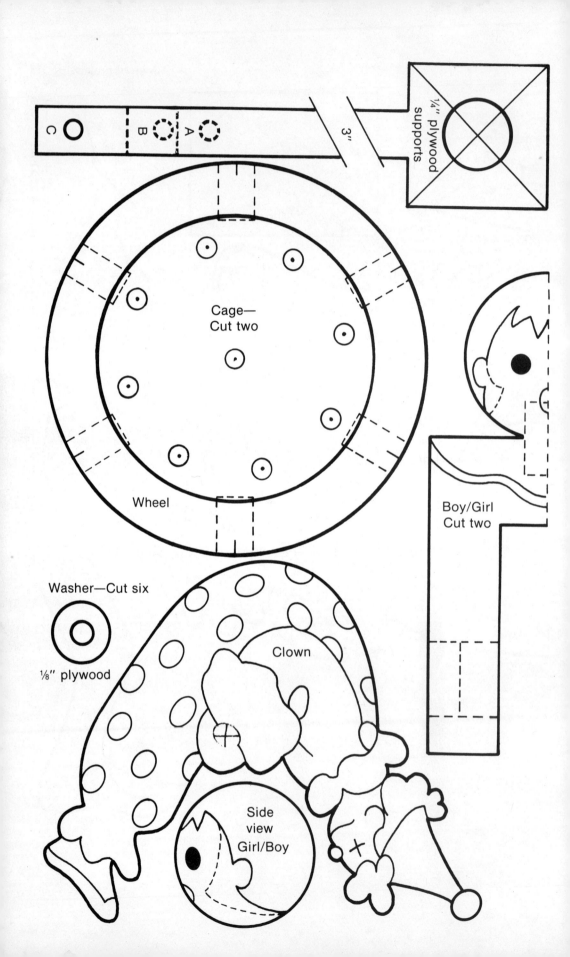

C O

B

A

3"

¼" plywood
supports

Cage—
Cut two

Wheel

Boy/Girl
Cut two

Washer—Cut six

⅛" plywood

Clown

Side
view
Girl/Boy

MUG HOLDER

Materials:

Top drawer:
  Back—$\frac{1}{4}$″ × 2″ × $9\frac{3}{8}$″
  Front—$\frac{1}{2}$″ × 2″ × $9\frac{3}{8}$″
  Ends—$\frac{1}{2}$″ × 2″ × 3″ (cut two)
  Bottom—$\frac{1}{2}$″ × 3″ × $8\frac{3}{8}$″
Bottom Drawer:
  Back and Front—$\frac{1}{2}$″ × 2″ × $9\frac{3}{8}$″ (cut two)
  Ends—$\frac{1}{2}$″ × 2″ × $2\frac{7}{8}$″ (cut two)
  Bottom—$\frac{1}{4}$″ × $2\frac{7}{8}$″ × $8\frac{3}{8}$″
Shelves—$\frac{1}{2}$″ × 4″ × $9\frac{1}{2}$″ (cut three)
Dividers—$\frac{1}{2}$″ × 4″ × $9\frac{3}{8}$″
Sides—$\frac{1}{2}$″ × 4″ × $14\frac{1}{2}$″ (cut two)

Back—$\frac{1}{4}$″ × $10\frac{1}{2}$″ × $15\frac{1}{2}$″
Coffee Mill:
  Back—2″ × 4″ × 8″
  Face—$\frac{1}{4}$″ × 4″ × 8″
Handle—1″ × 4″ × 8″
Porcelain knobs—1″ (two)
Touch latch

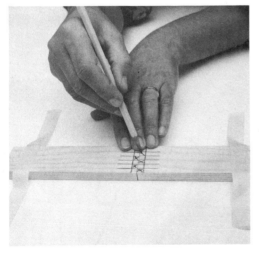

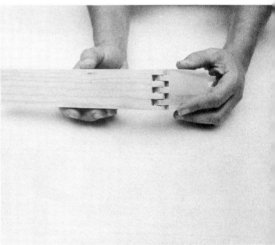

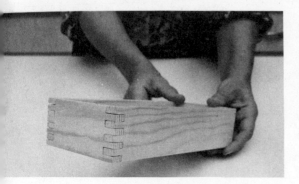

This mug holder has two drawers: one with mortise and tenon joints, which is visible, and one with butt joints, fastened with a touch latch, which is concealed. Back of drawer must be cut out to clear latch. Center shelf and vertical divider cross lap, and must be notched (½" × 2") for this purpose. White porcelain knobs are used on bottom drawer and coffee mill handle.

To install coffee mill, center it on top of mug holder and draw a pencil line around it. Drill two ¼" dowel holes 1" from each end of pencilled outline. Insert dowel markers in each hole and press mill piece down on them to line up holes. Drill holes in bottom of mill, insert dowel, and cut off to proper length. Glue decorative face to front of mill. Paint unit black to simulate metal. Use ¼" dowel to install handle in top of mill.

An easy way to mark the mortise and tenon for the bottom drawer is illustrated. Lay the sides end to end and place eight ¼" plywood strips on edge across each joint. Remove strips one by one, making a pencil mark each time. Then draw a line ½" in from the end of each piece. Mark pieces that are to be removed with an X and saw them out.

Note: See color photo on page 6 of insert.

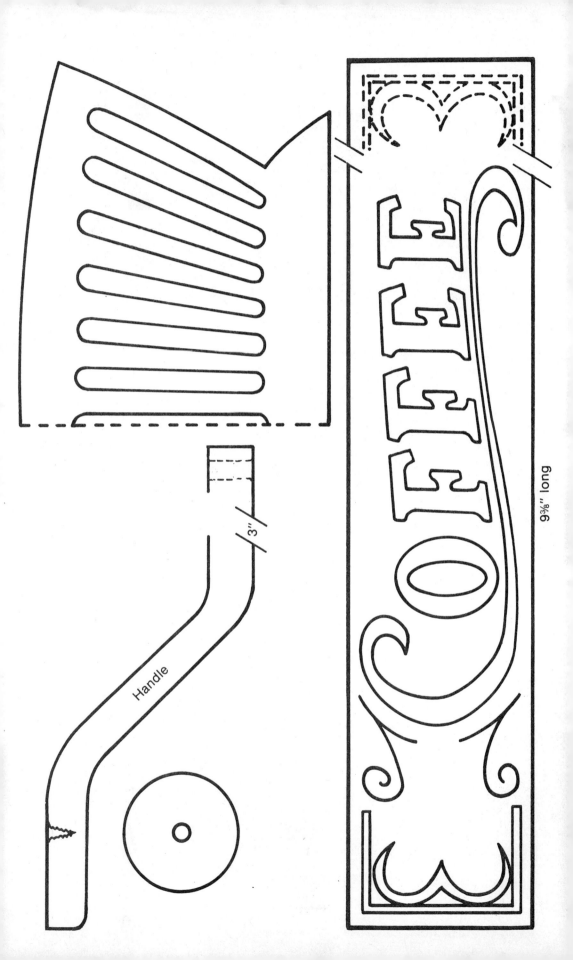

Handle

3"

9³⁄₈" long

THREE BEARS PULL TOY

Figures are ½" basswood, wagons 1" pine, wheels ¼" plywood, and axles ³⁄₁₆" dowel. Figures have extensions on feet to insert in slots because the feet are too fragile to drill for dowels. House is attached with dowel.

Note: See color photo on page 6 of insert.

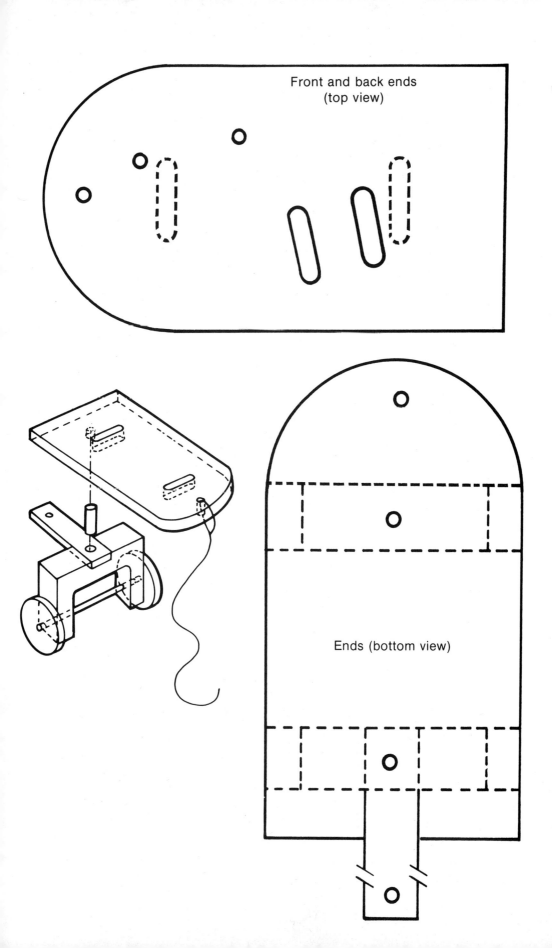

Front and back ends
(top view)

Ends (bottom view)

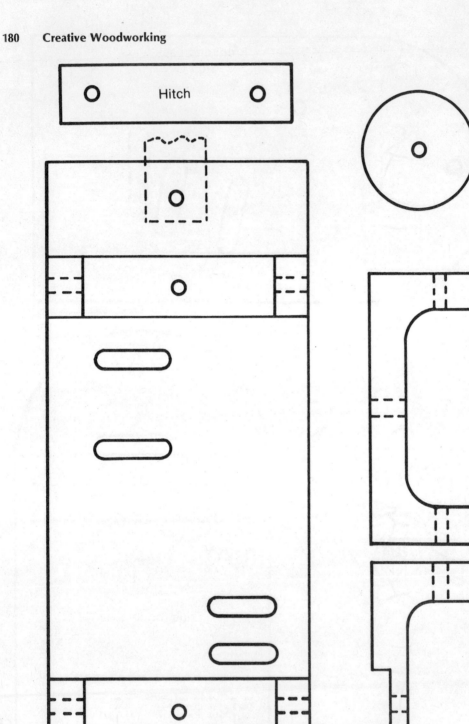

Hitch

NOAH'S ARK MOBILE

Materials:

> Figures and ark sides—⅛" plywood
> Ark center—1" pine
> Rainbow—⅜" plywood, ⅛" dowels
> Support—(see plan)

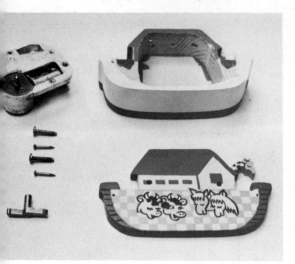
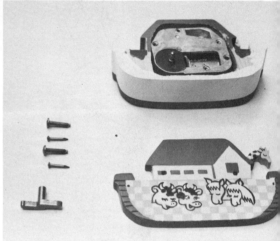

When tracing patterns use one giraffe head on one side of ark and second head on the other. Cut opening in center piece to fit music box. Drill hole for winding key in proper location. Glue one side in place and fasten other with small screws to permit access to music box for repairs.

Cut remaining pieces and drill all dowel holes as shown. Use Moto-Tool with #105 engraving cutter to drill tiny holes in top of figures for inserting strong invisible thread, using glue. Rainbow is

Outside view of attachment for crib mobile

Support for mobile

cross lap. Upper half has dove; lower half has sun from which ark is suspended with dowel.

Assemble project as illustrated. Ark alone makes delightful music box gift.

Note: See color photo on page 7 of insert.

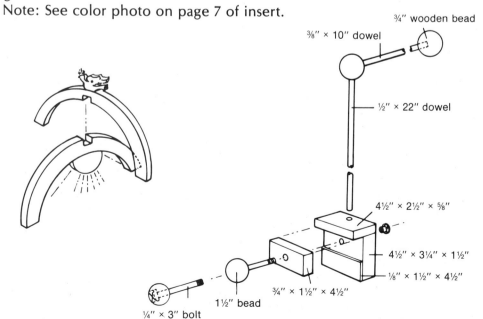

¾" wooden bead

⅜" × 10" dowel

½" × 22" dowel

4½" × 2½" × ⅝"

4½" × 3¼" × 1½"

⅛" × 1½" × 4½"

¾" × 1½" × 4½"

1½" bead

¼" × 3" bolt

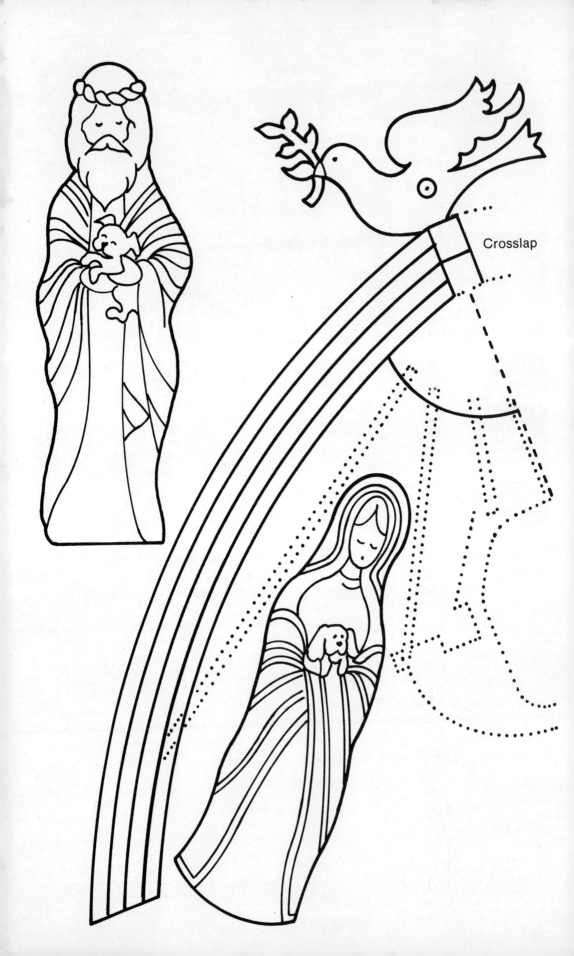

Crosslap

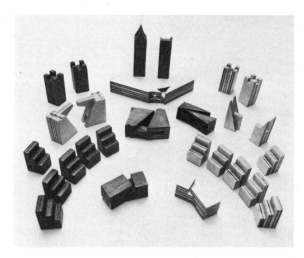

Designed by John Bernson

PORTABLE CHESS SET

This attractive chess set stores neatly in a box that is included in the carving section. It is cut from ¼" Baltic Birch plywood, but could be made from other plywood or solid stock. Simply cut the parts and glue them together as shown. Stain one set of chessmen dark and finish both sets with clear wood sealer.

Note: See color photo on page 6 of insert.

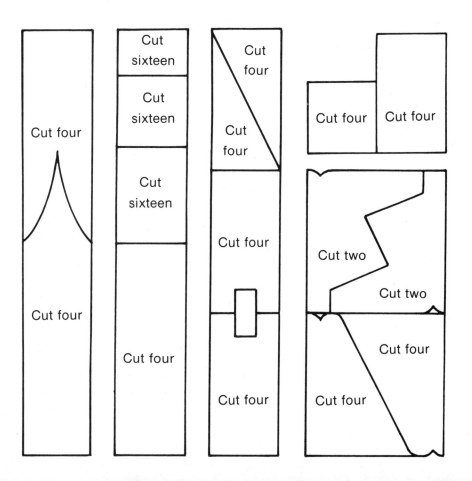

KANGAROO CHAIR

This rocking chair is made from ¾″ plywood. The jigsaw blade must be turned sideways to make the long cuts. The kangaroos require a piece 20″ × 26″; seat and back are 9½″ × 13½″. Assemble per diagram, using dowel kit to line up holes. Chair is intended for small child, one to three years old.

Note: See color photo on page 7 of insert.

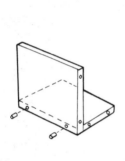

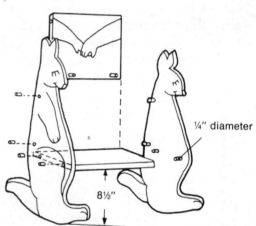

¼″ diameter

8½″

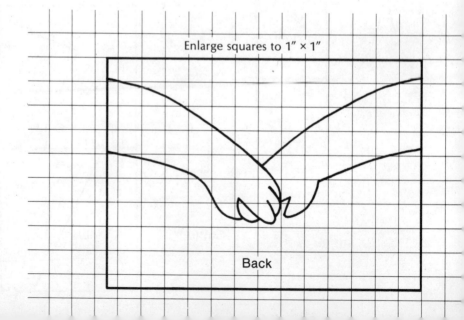

Enlarge squares to 1″ × 1″

Back

Side
Cut two

Enlarge squares to 1″ × 1″

ELEPHANT TEA CART

May be used by little ones for pretend tea-time or for lunch while watching television. Can also be used as an art center, with lower tray serving as storage area for crayons, coloring books, etc.

Cut sides from ⅜" plywood. Shelves are ⅜" plywood, 10" × 14" and 10" × 14¾". Attach ¼" × 1½" × 10" pieces to front and back ends of lower shelf. Attach 10" strips of decorative molding to front-top edge and back-top edge of upper tray. Cut wheels from 1" pine and join them with ⅜" dowel axles. Use ⅜" dowel for handle, 10¾" long.

Note: See color photo on page 7 of insert.

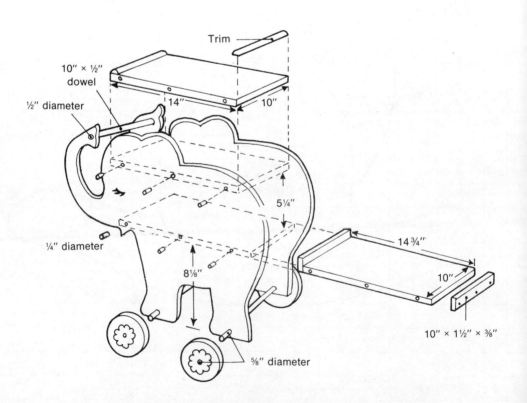

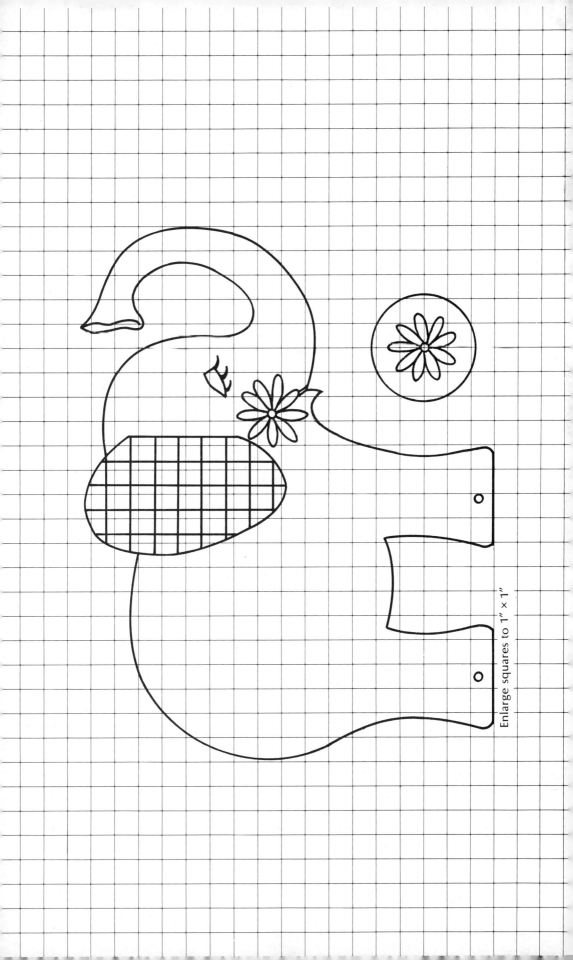

Enlarge squares to 1" × 1"

SOLDIER COAT RACK

Materials:

> Guardhouse—¼" plywood, 22" × 14"
> Inner soldier and base—⅜" plywood, 8" × 15"
> Outer soldier, front and ledge—⅛" plywood, 8" × 12"
> Dowels—⅛" and ⅜" (one 6" piece of each)
> Wooden balls or beads—¾" (three)
> Small wooden bead for flag (one)

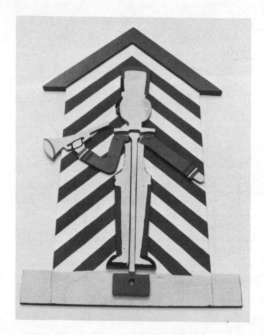

Sound the trumpet, wave the flag! That's what the soldier does when Johnny finally remembers to hang up his coat. The center coat peg activates a mechanism that raises both arms.

Create full-size soldier pattern by joining head and body patterns at neck joint. Trace full-size patterns on separate pieces of vellum or tracing paper. Enlarge guardhouse pattern and transfer it to ¼" plywood, including placement pattern for soldier's head and legs. Check accuracy and placement of patterns by laying them over the guardhouse pattern. Place inner leg pattern ⅛" above broken line; then add inner head pattern, which also shows location of actuator and dowels. Add actuator and full-size figure patterns. Be sure all line up exactly or the mechanism may not work.

Mark ⅛" dowel holes and drill. Cut inner head, inner legs, and inner front from ⅜" plywood; actuator, arms, and flag from ¼" plywood; full-size soldier, outer front, and ledge from ⅛" plywood.

Paint all pieces before assembling, except surfaces that will be glued or concealed. Assemble per diagram. Check mechanism to be sure it operates properly before gluing full-size soldier figure in place.

Note: See color photo on page 7 of insert.

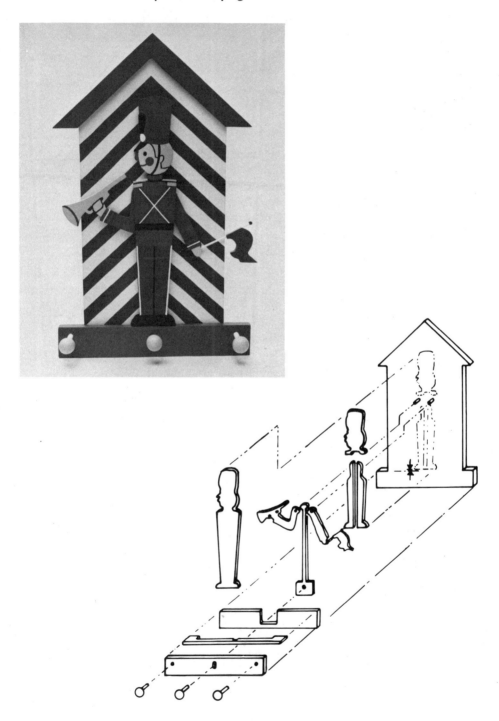

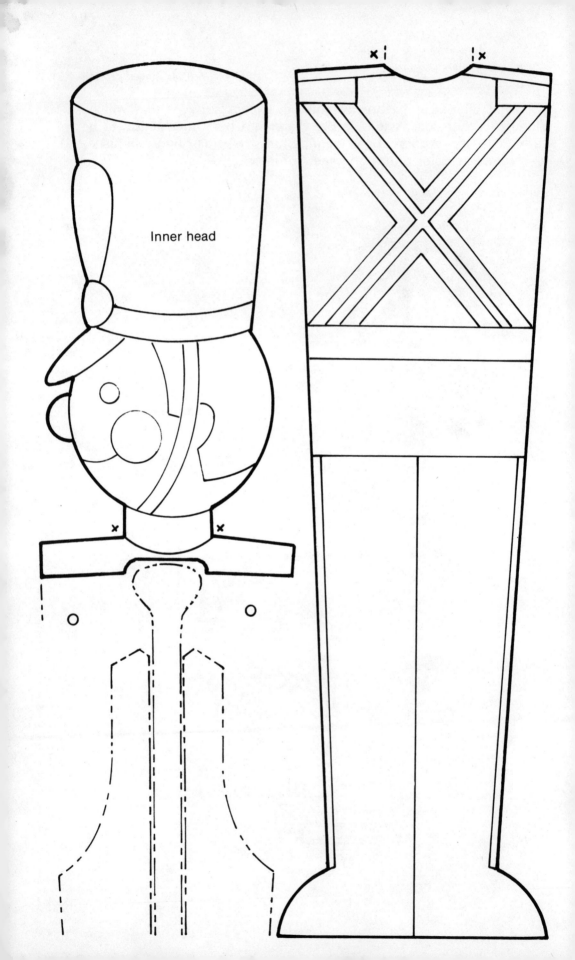

Inner head

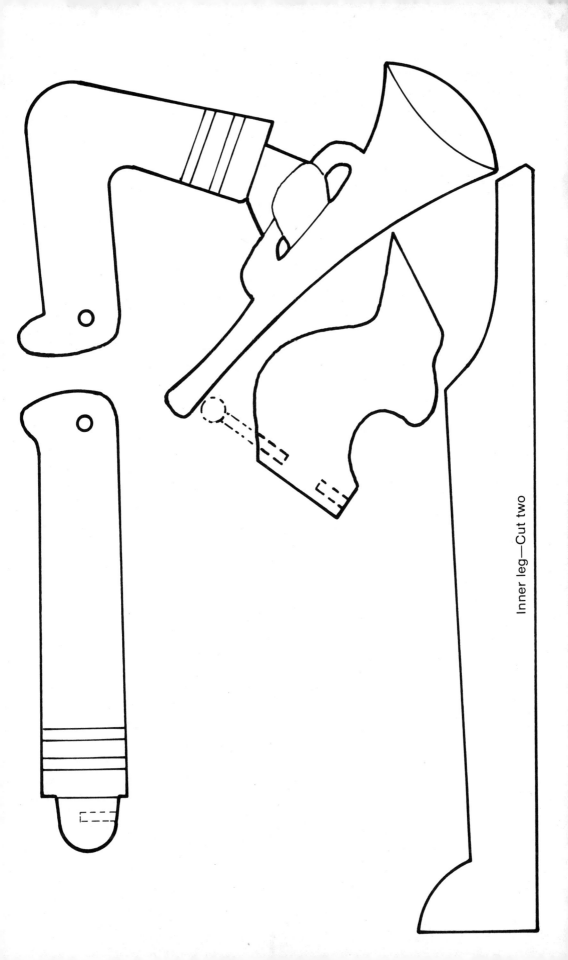

Inner leg—Cut two

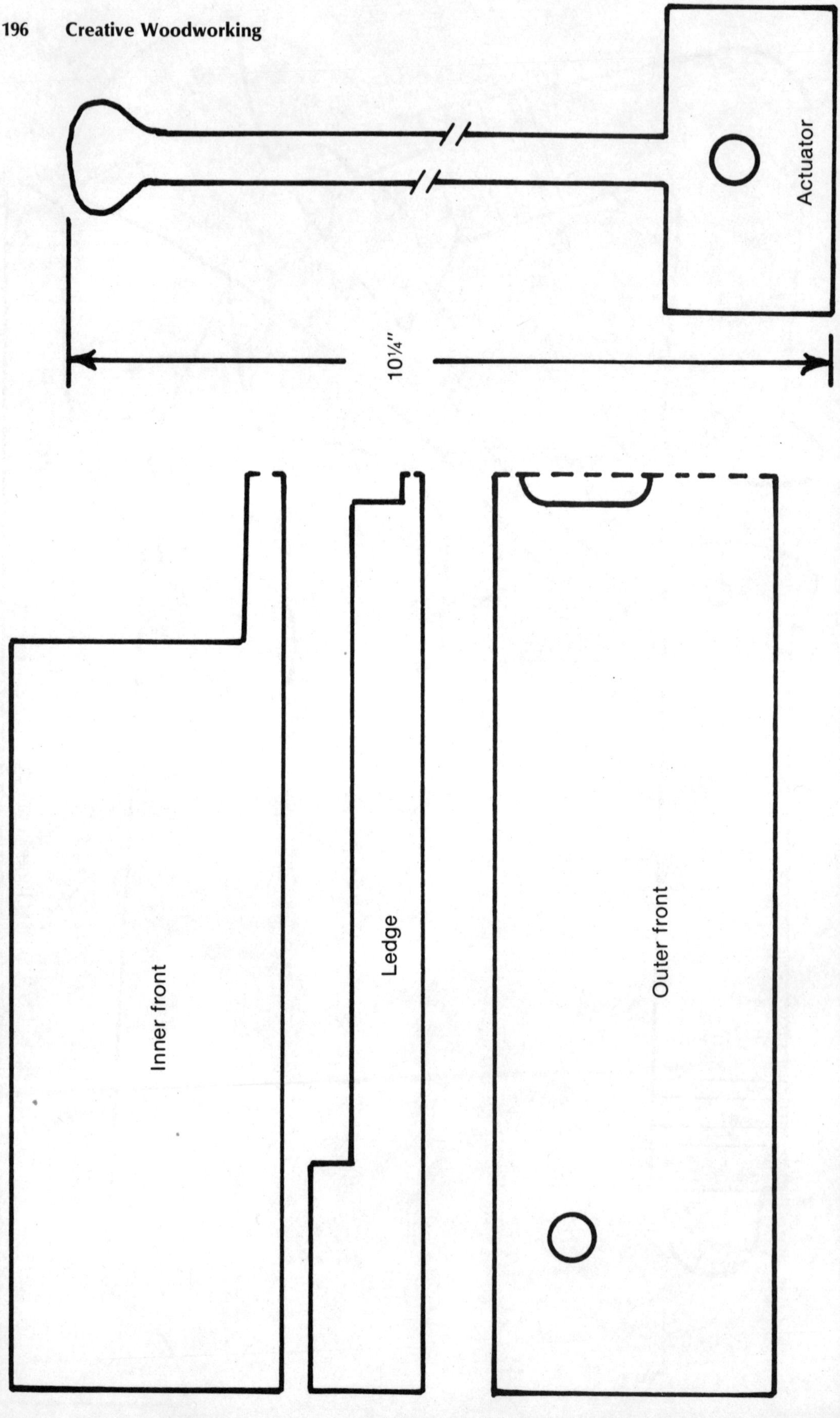

Actuator

10¼"

Inner front

Ledge

Outer front

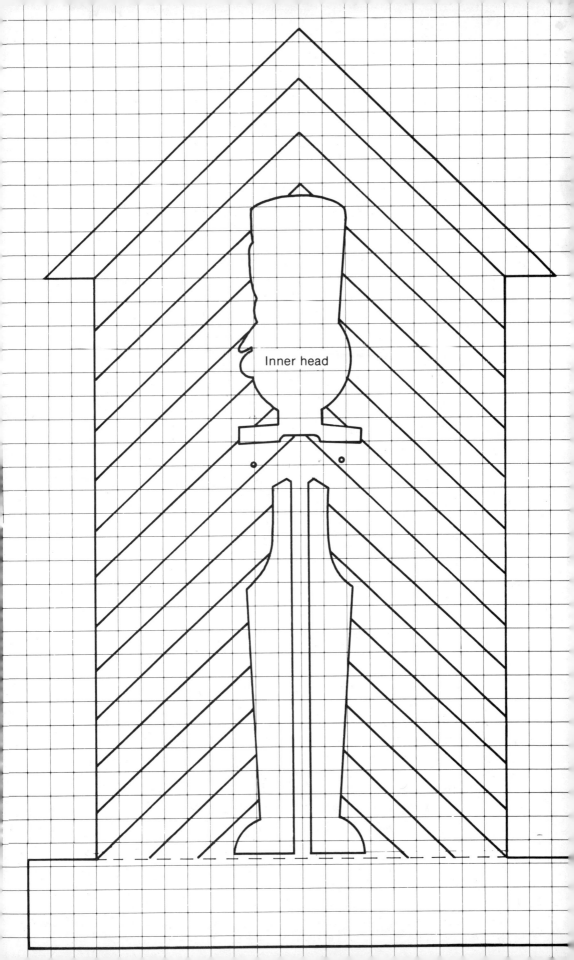

Inner head

GARDEN SHADOW BOX

Materials:

Box (use ½″ × 1½″ round edge stop):
    Top and bottom—1⅜″ × 10½″ (cut two)
    Sides—1″ × 1⅜″ × 11″ (cut two)
    Back—⅛″ plywood, 10½″ × 11″
Girls, flower pots, sprinkling can—¼″ plywood
Fence, lattice—⅛″ plywood
Flowers—¹⁄₁₆″ wood (or ⅛″ sanded down to ¹⁄₁₆″)

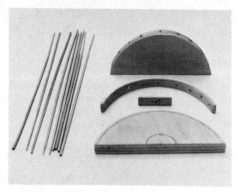

Parts for trellis

Using drum sander

Assemble box with butt joints and attach back with glue and small nails. Paint box before attaching any parts.

Cut and assemble trellis as shown in illustrations. Drill holes for spokes in outer edge of half-circle *before* cutting on jigsaw. Use #106 cutter on Moto-Tool or small hand drill bit. Then cut piece as shown and drill corresponding holes in small half-circle. Use bamboo shish kabob sticks for spokes. Allow spokes to protrude through outer rim, and cover with ⅛″ or ³⁄₁₆″ wooden beads. Glue pieces and hold firmly while they dry. Glue lattices as shown and install in upper corners of box. Glue trellis in place between them. Glue small pieces of ⅛″ plywood to back of hollyhocks, ¼″ pieces to back of standing girl, and ½″ pieces to back of kneeling girl. Install by gluing them to back of box in locations shown on floor plan. Assemble and glue fence in place, fitting it carefully between sides of box, ¼″ above the bottom and recessed ¼″.

Glue watering can and flower pots to fence at locations shown in

ssembling trellis (above)

Cutting leaves and flowers (left)

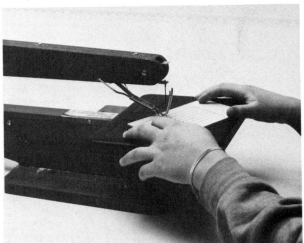

Cutting slats for fence (above)

Completed shadow box

floor plan. Paint leaves and flowers, and glue them to frame and lattices. Paint stems between them.

Illustrations show use of Moto-Tool holder and drum sander to smooth parts of trellis, and process for cutting fence and leaves and flowers. This technique is useful for any situation which requires you to cut many tiny pieces.

Note: See color photo on page 6 of insert.

GARDEN SHADOW BOX FLOOR PLAN

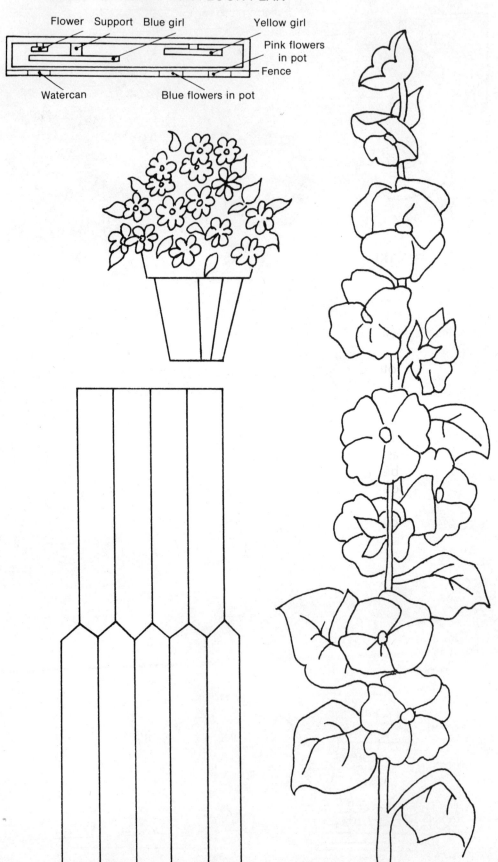

Flower   Support   Blue girl   Yellow girl

Pink flowers
in pot

Fence

Watercan   Blue flowers in pot

CHRISTMAS CARD HOLDER

Plywood ¼″ (20″ × 30″):
  Back—7″ × 28″
  Sides—3″ × 18″ (cut two)
  Pocket fronts—3″ × 6″ (cut three)
          5½″ × 6″ (cut one)
  Pocket bottoms—1″ × 5½″ (cut three)
          ¾″ × 5½″ (cut one)

Display your Christmas cards, with Santa's help, in this colorful Christmas card holder.

Assemble as shown. Glue sides and pocket bottoms to back and paint interior before attaching front pieces. Bevel edges slightly by sanding to produce perfect fit. Continue painted brick-pattern around sides.

Note: See color photo on page 7 of insert.

28"

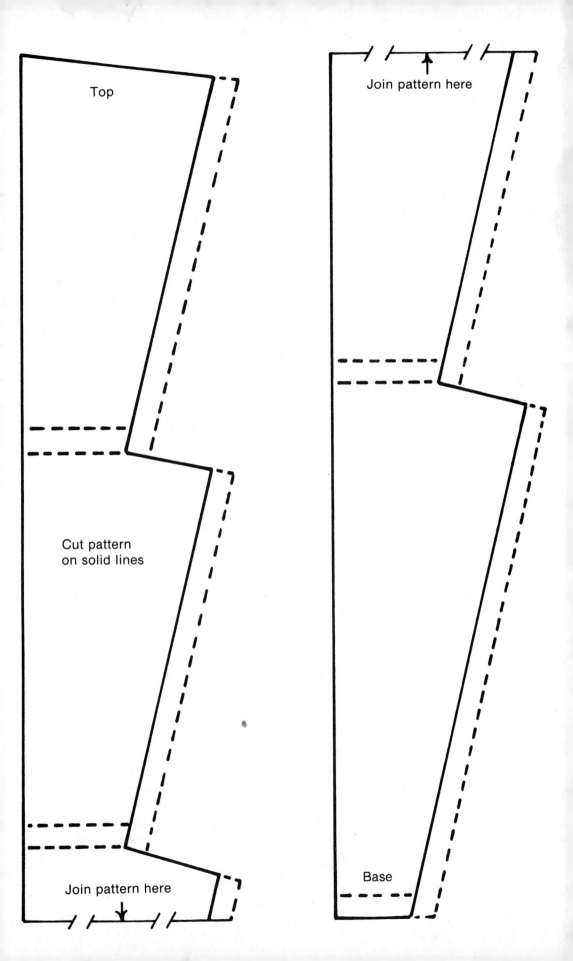

Top

Cut pattern
on solid lines

Join pattern here

Join pattern here

Base

STAY-IN-BED TRAY

Materials:

Frame:
  Ends—$3/4'' \times 3/4'' \times 16''$, ends mitered 45° (cut two)
  Front and back—$3/4'' \times 3/4'' \times 25''$, ends mitered 45° (cut two)
  Dividers—$3/4'' \times 3/4'' \times 15''$ (cut two)
  Base pieces—$3/8'' \times 4\frac{1}{2}'' \times 16''$ (cut two)
  Separators for handle opening—$3/8'' \times 3/4'' \times 6\frac{1}{4}''$ (cut two)
  Trim—$1/2'' \times 15\frac{3}{4}''$
  Ends—mitered 45° (cut two)
     Front and back—$1/2'' \times 24\frac{3}{4}''$, mitered 45° (cut two)
     Dividers—$1/2'' \times 15\frac{1}{4}''$, double mitered 45° (cut two)
  Dowels—$1/4'' \times 15''$ (cut seven)
        $1/4'' \times 9''$ (cut fifty)
        $1/4'' \times 7\frac{1}{2}''$ (cut six)
Removable Tray:
  Ends—$1/2'' \times 1\frac{1}{2}'' \times 14\frac{1}{4}''$, mitered 45° (cut two)
  Front and back—$1/2'' \times 1\frac{1}{2}'' \times 15\frac{5}{8}''$, mitered 45° (cut two)
  Bottom—$1/8'' \times 13\frac{1}{2}'' \times 14\frac{7}{8}''$
  Dowel—$3/16'' \times 2''$ (cut eight)

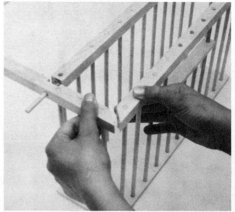

If your child is confined to bed with the measles or mumps, you'll both be happier if he has this stay-in-bed tray to use. The cup holder is perfect for crayons or a glass of water for his watercolor set. The baskets on the side will hold toys and coloring books. Moms and dads will enjoy the tray, too, for breakfast in bed.

Complete half-pattern for base and frame. Use as guide for marking dowel holes and positioning dividers. To insure that dowel holes line up exactly, be sure to drill matching pieces simultaneously.

After drilling first and second holes, insert a dowel to assure continued alignment. Note that the handle-opening separator contains three blind dowel-holes. Drill evenly spaced blind dowel holes for horizontal dowels that support removable tray. Assemble and glue stand for tray as illustrated in the photos.

Enlarge half-pattern for tray sides and handles. Cut remaining

 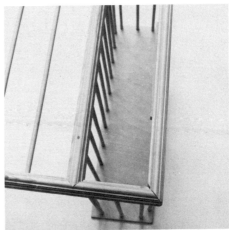

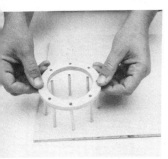 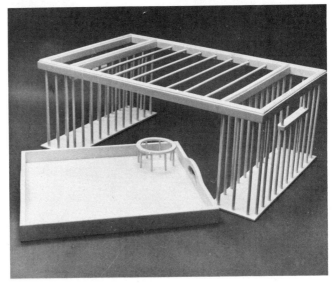

pattern pieces. Drill holes in ring and tray bottom. Rout sides using table saw or Moto-Tool. Complete assembly by gluing bottom and joining corners with countersunk fine nails.

Note: See color photo on page 7 of insert.

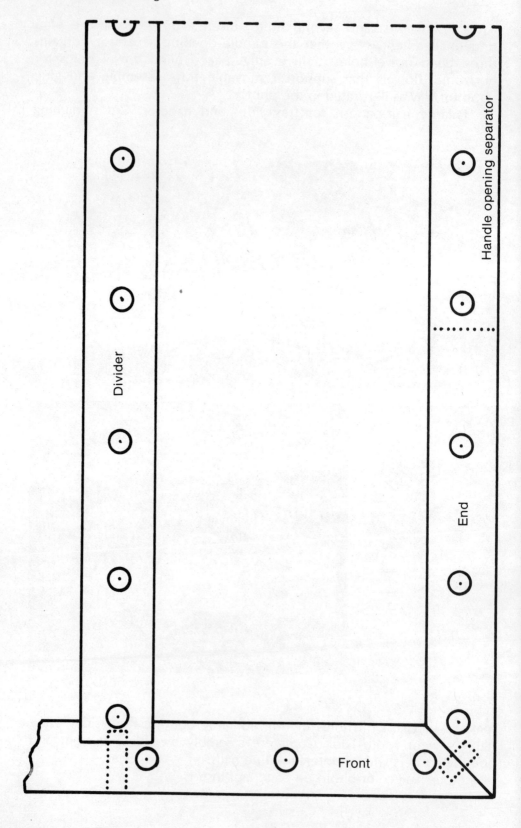

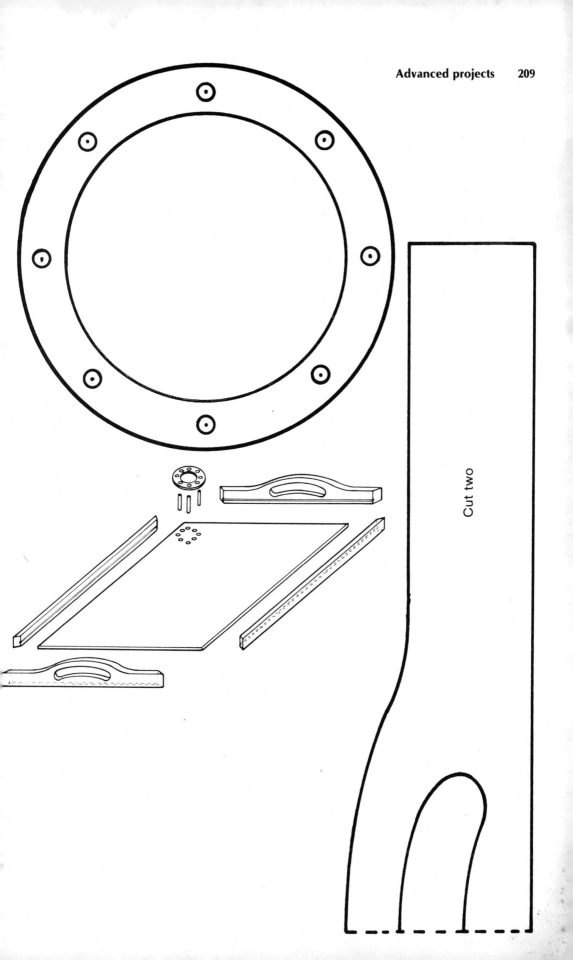

Cut two

GINGERBREAD HOUSE

Children are fascinated by the secret lock on this colorful gingerbread house, which is also a bank. The mystery is in the door, which must be moved to the right and upward so you can slide the bottom out to remove your savings. The ice-cream cones and candy pieces on the roof conceal the coin slots. The house is cut from ¼" plywood and the applied pieces from ⅛" plywood.

Assemble pieces as shown in diagram (figures 13 and 15–18 in chapter 3 were taken during construction of the "Gingerbread House"), using glue and fine nails. Note that sides must be beveled at angle of roof. Front and back extend over sides; so side painting pattern covers front and back edges, as well. Be sure to check lock mechanism to see that it works properly before gluing the parts together.

Note: See color photo on page 8 of insert.

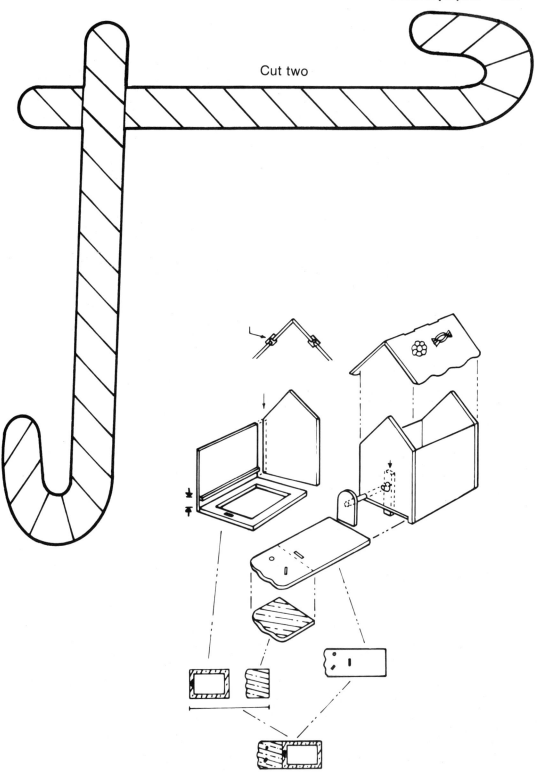

Cut two

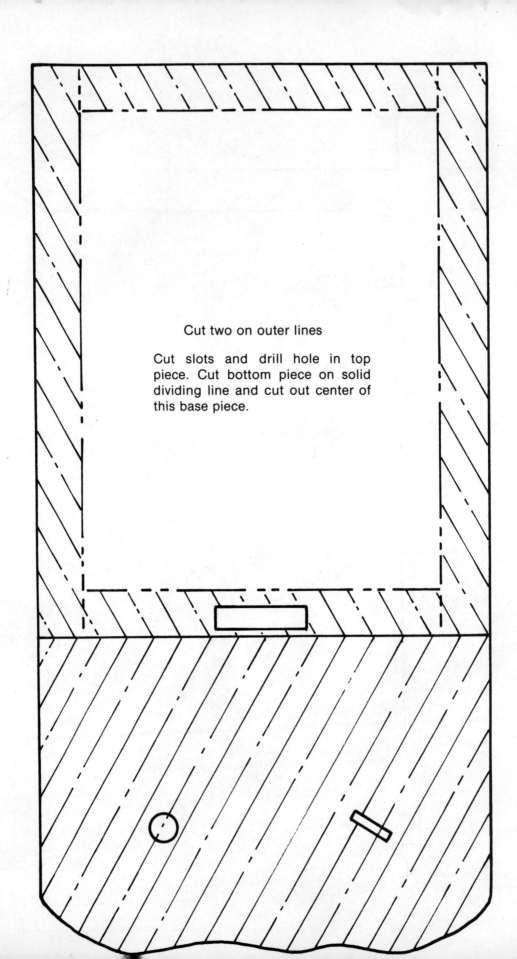

Cut two on outer lines

Cut slots and drill hole in top piece. Cut bottom piece on solid dividing line and cut out center of this base piece.

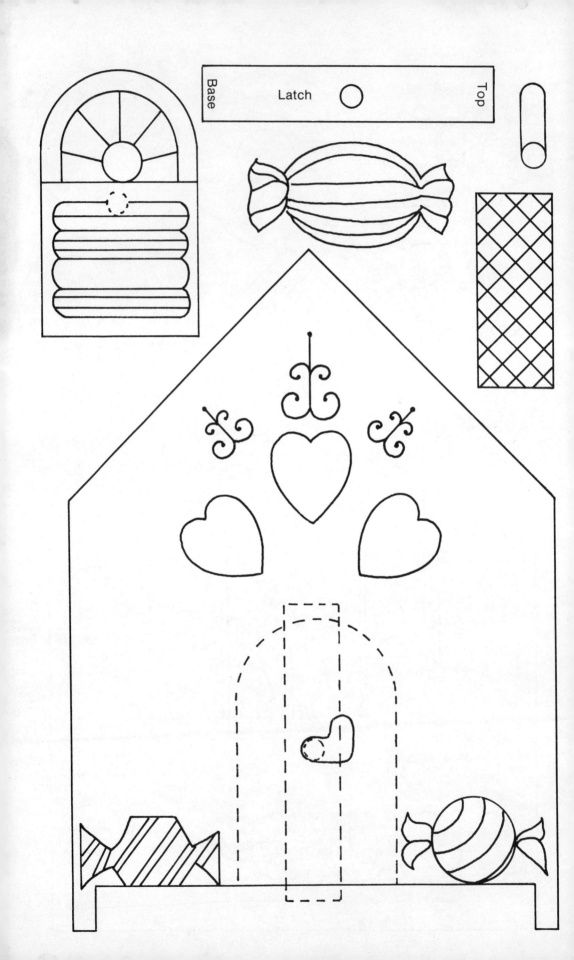

Base   Latch   Top

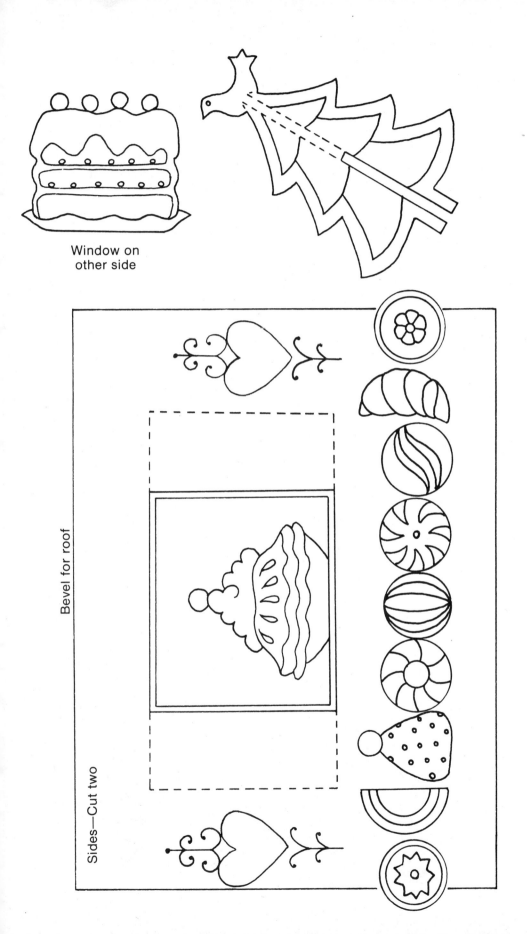

Window on
other side

Bevel for roof

Sides—Cut two

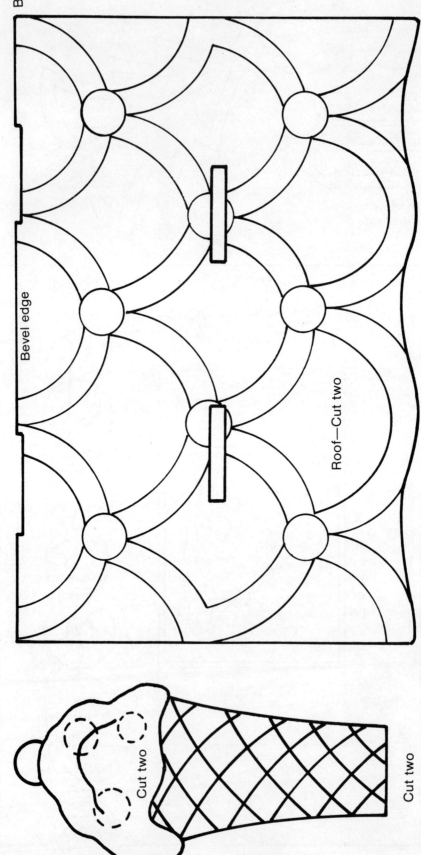

Bevel

Bevel edge

Roof—Cut two

Cut two

Cut two

CAT CHOW BOX

Here's a challenge for you! Cut parts and assemble as indicated in diagram. Handle is a reduction of pattern for "Tiger Tape Holder," but you can use any figure you choose, or a simple knob. If you plan to use container for cookies or candy instead of cat food, use gingerbread boy or girl for knob and decorate with designs from gingerbread house.

Note: See color photo on page 8 of insert.

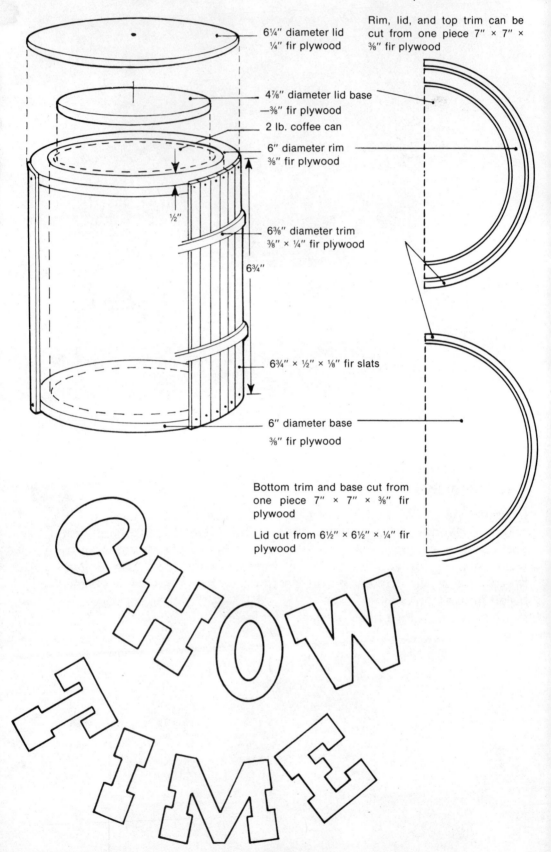

6¼" diameter lid
¼" fir plywood

4⅞" diameter lid base
—⅜" fir plywood

2 lb. coffee can

6" diameter rim
⅜" fir plywood

½"

6⅜" diameter trim
⅜" × ¼" fir plywood

6¾"

6¾" × ½" × ⅛" fir slats

6" diameter base
⅜" fir plywood

Cutting directions
Top view

Rim, lid, and top trim can be cut from one piece 7" × 7" × ⅜" fir plywood

Bottom trim and base cut from one piece 7" × 7" × ⅜" fir plywood

Lid cut from 6½" × 6½" × ¼" fir plywood

CHOW
TIME

17 Introduction to woodcarving

Basic instructions on carving with the Moto-Tool were provided in chapter 5, but before you begin the projects in this section a few rules should be underscored:

1. Study the safety precautions in chapter 2 and observe them faithfully.
2. Hold the Moto-Tool as you would a pencil and keep it at a 45° angle.
3. Always move the tool from right to left.
4. Don't exert too much pressure. Take your time and let the tool do the work. If the wood begins to smoke, you're pressing too hard.
5. Cut with the grain; don't fight the wood.
6. Don't gouge too deeply in a single cut; let the tool chew the wood away a little at a time.

The simplest form of carving is *incised line carving*. It requires no artistic talent; the carver simply follows the pattern line on the wood and etches out the design. The outlined form remains at the same level as the background. An example is shown in Figure 39. *Incised carving* is somewhat more elaborate, in that the separation between the outline and the background is emphasized by broadening and sloping the background side of the outline. The mane of the rocking horse carved on the purchased box shown here is an example.

The process is carried one step further in *intaglio carving*, which is really relief carving in reverse. Instead of raising the carved design above the background surface, it is carved to the same depth below the surface. If a piece were cast from an intaglio carving it would duplicate the same pattern carved in raised relief.

In *low relief carving* the pattern is outlined with a stop cut, and the background is then carved away. That's what Bob Johannes is

doing on the zodiac plaque shown here. A full set of zodiac patterns can be obtained from many Dremel dealers or from the Dremel manufacturer. Much "country carving" is low relief carving.

   High relief carving is more intricate and difficult, approaching three-dimensional carving (carving in-the-round) in the level of skill required. The designs are cut deeper and undercut to the point that they appear to be detached from the background. Both the surface and the sides of the design are carved.

   Finally—and this is where native talent is revealed—there is *three-dimensional carving,* in which the eye must be trained to judge contours, dimensions, and proportions. Sample projects, some designed by Bob Johannes, are included in this book. Try a few and then strike out on your own to design and carve subjects that have particular appeal to you.

If this is your first experience with the Moto-Tool, some practice on scraps of wood is advisable before you undertake your first project. The 381 kit includes two cutters: a high speed cutter and a small engraving cutter. These will get you started, but you will want to add others as you attempt the projects that follow.

Begin your practice session by inserting the #131 cutter in the Moto-Tool. Unscrew the chuck cap, thread the cutter through it and into the collet, and then replace the chuck cap. Push in the locking pin and tighten the chuck with the wrench that is provided. About ½" of the cutter should protrude from the cap.

Be sure to rest your arm on a flat surface and maneuver the Moto-Tool with your fingers. You may find that this makes you more comfortable and allows better control of the tool. When you are working near the outer edge of the design, rest your arm on another board the same thickness as the one you are carving. Take your time, relax, and rest if you become tense because your fingers are tired. With a little practice you'll be carving with skill and ease.

Hold the tool with your thumb and forefinger placed firmly on the plastic end of the tool just above the chuck. The tool will rest easily in the curvature between thumb and finger. Hold the Moto-

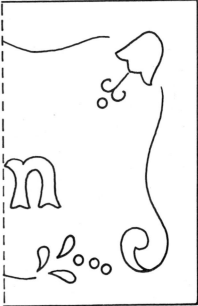

Tool at a 45° angle and cut a shallow groove in the wood, moving from right to left. Now try another stroke to deepen the groove further. Draw a pattern on the wood and try tracing it. Switch to the smaller #107 cutter and try carving a few lines.

When you get the feel of the tool, try the #107 cutter on some of the line carving patterns in the book. Use carbon paper to transfer the pattern to the wood. Work with the incised line carving patterns until you feel you have mastered this technique.

When you have completed your first simple relief carving and have applied the stain, you probably will find that some lines are less sharply defined than others. Usually, this is because they were not carved deeply enough. Don't despair; simply recarve these lines to the proper depth and apply another coat of stain. Don't leave it on too long, however, or you may have a dark spot on the surface of the board.

Now try low relief carving, using the "Joy, Love, and Peace" plaque pattern. Trace the pattern on $\frac{3}{8}$" or $\frac{1}{2}$" basswood and go over it with a felt tip pen so the lines stand out.

Next, use the #107 cutter to cut all outlines down to the $\frac{1}{8}$" depth. Then switch to the #131 cutter and remove the background wood to the same depth. Work outward from the edges of the design using short strokes and following the grain as much as possible. When the background has been removed, go back to the #107 cutter to clean out tight areas and carve in the detail. Then use the drum sander to create a more finished appearance by rounding the edges of the pattern. Finally, sand the surface of the design with fine abrasive paper, and lightly sand the background. How smooth you make it is a matter of personal preference. In most cases the background will be left quite rough because the chiseled effect enhances the work.

When you have finished carving and sanding, clean the work carefully with a soft brush and cloth. Finish it as desired, using stain or simply applying three coats of semi-gloss clear wood-finish. Go over each coat lightly with very fine abrasive paper or 0000 steel wool before applying another coat

Use the chart and table that follow "Dremel Moto-Tool Accessories" as a guide in the selection of the appropriate Moto-Tool accessory for the job at hand. Patterns for a number of plaques, to be carved in both simple and raised relief, have been included. Try them on basswood or sugar pine before moving on to more ambitious projects.

You will discover, when cutting these soft woods, that the sawdust and shavings tend to obscure the pattern. Keep a brush handy to remove debris as you work. Be sure to sand the wood before you begin to carve, and observe the grain when you place your pattern.

When some woods are stained—pine among them—the grain becomes more pronounced. Your pattern should be placed so that the grain of the wood will enhance your finished carving, not detract from it.

As you begin carving, don't overlook the potential of the Moto-Shop and Moto-Tool for making objects to carve. If you want to carve a block too thick to cut on the Moto-Shop, make your own block by using the Moto-Shop to cut several pieces that can be glued together. This can produce some interesting grain variations, but for ease of carving be sure that all of the pieces are placed with the grain running in the same direction.

You can design and make your own plaques, boxes, and other objects, cutting them on the jigsaw and using the Moto-Tool with router attachment to decorate the edges. Use the principles already outlined to make round boxes, using the Moto-Tool drum sander to finish the insides and to carve the exteriors. The variety that you can introduce into your carving will be limited only by your own creativity and imagination.

Examine the jigsaw projects in this book to determine those you would like to enhance with carving. The Thanksgiving plaque could be given a routed edge; other projects, on which pieces were applied to simulate carving, could be carved instead. The design on the onion box could be carved in raised relief, and the coffee grinder on the mug holder would be more realistic if it were shaped and carved.

Rings rough cut on jigsaw and glued together to form interesting shapes for carving or painting

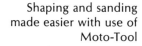

Shaping and sanding made easier with use of Moto-Tool

Remember, though, not to carve plywood unless you desire an effect from the contrasting layers of wood. Substitute solid stock and use thicker material if necessary, adjusting measurements of other parts to conform.

Note: See color photo on page 8 of insert.

DREMEL MOTO-TOOL ACCESSORIES

Each project you undertake is unique; therefore the applications listed are intended as general guidelines only. The versatility of each accessory is limited only by your imagination and experience.

General Caution: It is mandatory that safety glasses and dust mask be worn by anyone operating or viewing the operation of a Moto-Tool. Flying particles could cause injury!

Cutters (grouped by shape)

All cutter sizes in the same shape group will accomplish the same basic cut. Cutters of the same shape are sometimes made from different substances to cut different materials (see Dremel Cutter Table). Cutter size determines the width and depth of a cut, and also the degree of detail which may be accomplished.

Cylinders: Used for lines, grooves, channels, angular cuts, flat-bottom cuts, and square cuts.

Balls: Used for cuts where sharp corners are not required. Will result in radius cuts, such as pockets, radius background for relief carvings, and grooves. Small sizes may be used for moderate line work and veining.

Pears, Ovals: Similar to group 2. More desirable for deep and wide grooving, concaving and rounding, and gradual curves.

Flames, Christmas Trees: Used for veining, deep narrow V grooves, undercuts, and outside radii.

Slotting Cutters: Used for narrow slotting and channeling where sharp corners are required.

Grinding and sanding

There are numerous shapes and sizes of mounted wheel points. Different points are ideal for sharpening, deburring, and general purpose grinding; specific uses are determined by project application. Sanding accessories that are ideal for general shaping and smoothing are also available. The guidelines listed below should be followed when determining which grinding or sanding accessory group is best for specific materials.

Note: All grinding wheels must be "dressed" prior to initial use and periodically during use. *Dressing* is the process of removing any out of round on a grinding wheel by holding a dressing stone against its surface while it is spinning. This will result in smoother grinding with minimum bounce. Dremel dressing stone part no. 415 is recommended.

Aluminum Oxide: Should be used when application involves steel, all non-ferrous metals, plastics, bone, shell, "green" ceramics. Note: Non-ferrous metals have a tendency to clog grinding surface and will necessitate frequent dressing of wheel.

Silicon Grinding Points: Should be used when application involves hardened steel, "fired" ceramics, glass, shell, stone, and other very hard materials.

Sanding Drums and Discs: Should be used when application involves wood, fiberglass, or bone. Note: Fiberglass is an extremely abrasive material and can result in damage to Moto-Tool bearings if dust enters tool.

Cleaning and Polishing

Polishing, buffing, and brushing are methods employed to clean, or renew lustre to various surfaces. Caution: When polishing, buffing, or brushing plated material, extreme caution must be used or the plated surface will be removed; thus exposing the undersurface and ruining the project.

Polishing: Consists of rubber wheels which are impregnated with a very fine abrasive. Removes more material than buffing and should be used *prior* to buffing for initial smoothing of a rough surface. Used on materials such as steel, non-ferrous metals, precious metals, glass, plastics (use very light pressure or plastic will melt), stone, bone, and shells.

Buffing: Contains fabric wheels and points which must be impregnated with an abrasive such as Dremel polishing compound no. 421 or jeweler's rouge, and removes less material than polishing, resulting in a higher lustre than polishing. Can be used without prior polishing on smooth surfaces. Used on materials such as steel, non-ferrous metals, precious metals, glass, plastic (use very light pressure or plastic will melt), stone, bone, and shells.

Brushing: Used for removal of rust, corrosion, dirt, etc., from base material, which includes steel, non-ferrous metals, precious metals, and glass. Can be used to texture wood, plastics, bone, and shells. Caution: Brushes should not be operated at speeds exceeding 15,000 RPM. At higher speeds bristles may become detached and injure the user.

Sawing

Use for slicing, cutting off, slotting, and similar operations.

Steel Saws: Used on wood, plastics, fiberglass, bone, plaster, and linoleum.

Cutting Wheel: An abrasive impregnated wheel used on hard and soft steel and non-ferrous metals.

Caution: Due to the extreme cutting action of these accessories, protective gloves should be worn at all times. The Moto-Tool should be held with both hands during cutting operation.

Dremel Woodcarving Accessories

124 4	100 2	114 2	121 4
144 3	131 3	134 3	141 3
189 2	105 2	106 2	107 2
193 1	190 2	191 2	192 2
116 1	194 1	196 1	115 1
125 4	117 3	178 5	118 4
	197 5	198 5	199 5

Part numbers (lower left) and group numbers (lower right) are used on "Dremel Cutter Table"

DREMEL CUTTER TABLE

	Cylinders Group 1.	Balls Group 2.	Pear, Oval Group 3.	Flame Xmas Tree Group 4.	Slotting Group 5.
High Speed Cutters*— Wood, Soft Metals, Plastics, Bone, and Some Shells	193 194 196 115 116	100 114 189 190 191 192	131 134 141 144 117	121 124 118 125	178 197 198 199
Tungsten Carbide Cutters—Hard and Soft Metals, Plastics, Glass, Bone, Most Shells, Ceramics, and Some Stone	9901 9902 9912	9905 9906	9903 9904 9907	9908 9909 9910 9911	
Small Engraving Cutters— Wood, Plastics, Bone, and Some Shells	108 109 110 111 112 113	105* 106* 107*			

SUGGESTED SPEEDS

Maximum Speed (25,000 to 30,000 RPM)—Glass, shells, stone, hard metals and wood.
Moderate Speed (15,000 to 25,000 RPM)—Wood, soft metals, thermoset plastic.
Slow Speed (8,000 to 15,000 RPM)—Soft metals, thermoplastics.

*See Dremel Woodcarving Accessories diagrams.

DISCO BAG

The "in" gadget for carrying lipstick and "mad money" during an evening on the town. Use this design or create one of your own. Trace oval pattern on one piece of 1" solid stock and two pieces of 1/8" solid stock. Use #107 engraving cutter on Moto-Tool to rout a groove around side of 1" oval. Transfer pattern to one or both 1/8" ovals and carve with #105 engraving cutter. Separate 1" oval as indicated. Mark and drill 3/32" holes. Cut out center as shown. Glue 1/8" sides to larger half of 1" oval. Insert top half and sand edges. Stain and spray with clear wood sealer. Thread cord through holes as shown.

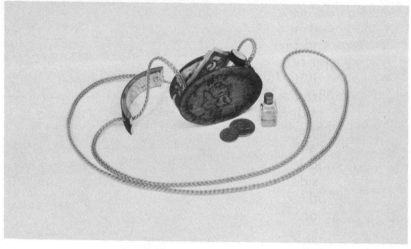

CHESS BOOK

Materials:

Basswood ⅛″:
  Top and bottom—5½″ × 6¾″ (cut two)
  Drawer bottom—4⅝″ × 5⅝″
  Sides of drawer—1″ × 6¼″ (cut two) (A)
  False front of drawer—1″ × 5³⁄₁₆″ (C)
  Ends of drawer—1″ × 4⅝″ (cut two) (B)
  Bottom end of book—1¹⁄₁₆″ × 5⅜″ (F)
  Outer side of book—1¹⁄₁₆″ × 6⅜″ (G)
Basswood ¼″:
  Spine side of book—1″ × 6¼″ (E)
Basswood ½″:
  Spine of book—1⅜″ × 6¾″ (D)

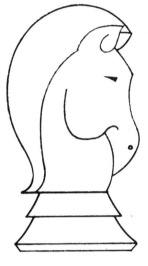

Store your portable chess set in this attractive box, which also serves as an interesting table decoration when carved with the Moto-Tool.

Assemble box per diagram. Sand and fit parts carefully so that drawer slides easily but fits snugly. Carve grooves at edge of binding with #131 cutter. Carve knight's head and roman numeral XXXII on spine with #106 engraving cutter. Use saw blade #406 to scribe sides of books to resemble pages.

Note: See color photo on page 8 of insert.

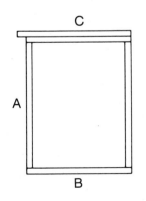

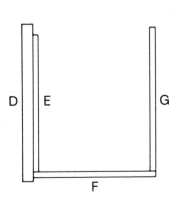

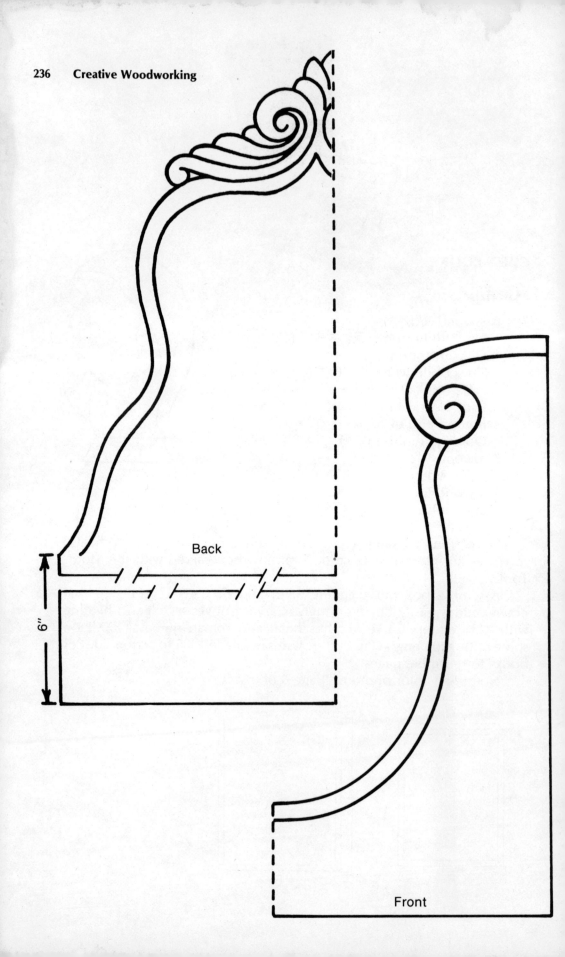

Back

6"

Front

IRON CADDY

Materials:

Basswood ½":
 Back—6" × 11¼"
 Front—6" × 6"
 Sides—4½" × 6" (cut two)
 Bottom—4½" × 5"

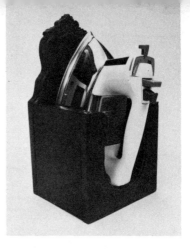

Store your iron neatly in this unusual iron caddy. Complete patterns and trace on front and back sections, including carving patterns. Cut parts including sides and bottom listed above. Carve large grooves with a #131 cutter and smaller grooves with a #107 engraving cutter. Stain, or paint as desired. This caddy is finished with Deft walnut spray-stain and three coats of clear wood finish, sanded with #400 abrasive paper between coats.

Note: See color photo on page 8 of insert.

UMBRELLA STAND

Here is a simple relief carving with an elaborate design that was adapted from a set of dinnerware. Use ½" basswood to cut four sides, 6" × 20", and an inset bottom, 5" × 5". Carve design with #106 engraving cutter. Use natural finish, or paint as desired.

Before applying stain check the color by first applying a small amount on the back of a board. Wipe off immediately. The longer you leave the stain on the darker it will become.

Carved umbrella stand (left) has mitered corners. Design would also make an interesting wall hanging.

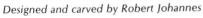

Designed and carved by Robert Johannes

GULLS

These attractive gulls can be used as pins, pendants, or decorative pieces. The rough blank is cut on the jigsaw, and the gull is shaped with the drum sander on the Moto-Tool. The base for the mobile can be cut on the jigsaw and the edge routed with the Moto-Tool. Drill tiny holes in the base and gulls with the #105 engraving cutter. Insert thin stiff wires to hold gulls, and glue in place. Use any hardwood with an attractive grain.

OWL BOLO

Cut blank from ¼" walnut. Shape with drum sander on Moto-Tool and cut detail with edge of #193 and #194 cutters. Cut holes for eyes with #106 cutter.

Designed and carved by Robert Johannes

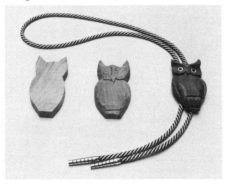

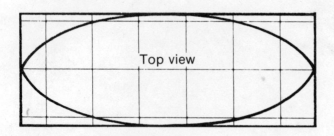

Top view

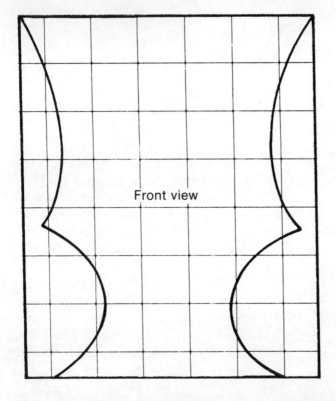

Front view

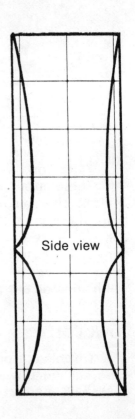

Side view

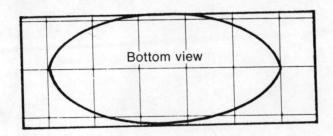

Bottom view

URN

Designed and carved by Robert Johannes

Use any hardwood. Urn is shaped with #194 cutter and drum sander. Rout inside opening with #196 and #134 cutters. This piece can also be made with a flat back for use as a wall hanging. Rough cut the side pattern on the jigsaw and shape the front side only.

HERON

This piece was done in butternut. Shape with drum sander. Use #144 cutter to cut grooves in base, #196 for feather cuts, #191 to cut opening under tail, and #106 to cut eye.

Note: See color photo on page 8 of insert.

Designed and carved by Robert Johannes

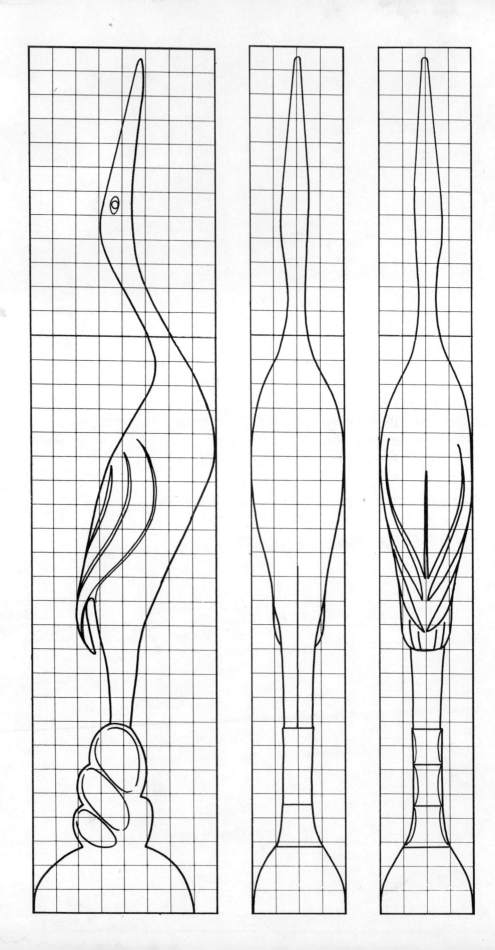

OWL

Designed and carved by Robert Johannes

Cut from basswood. Round off with #131 cutter. Use #110 cutter for feather cuts, #107 for wing line (tilted), #406 for hair lines on head, and gouge design in base with #134 cutter. Use appropriate size drill to make holes for purchased glass or plastic eyes.

Note: See color photo on page 8 of insert.

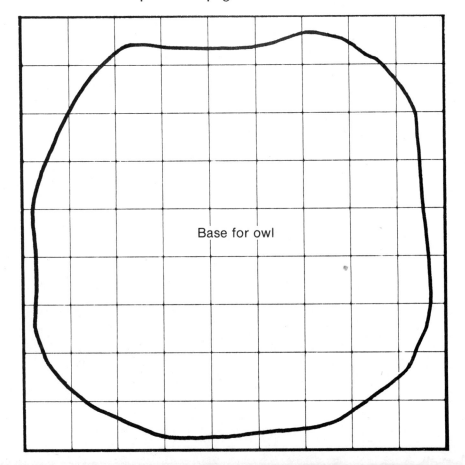

Base for owl

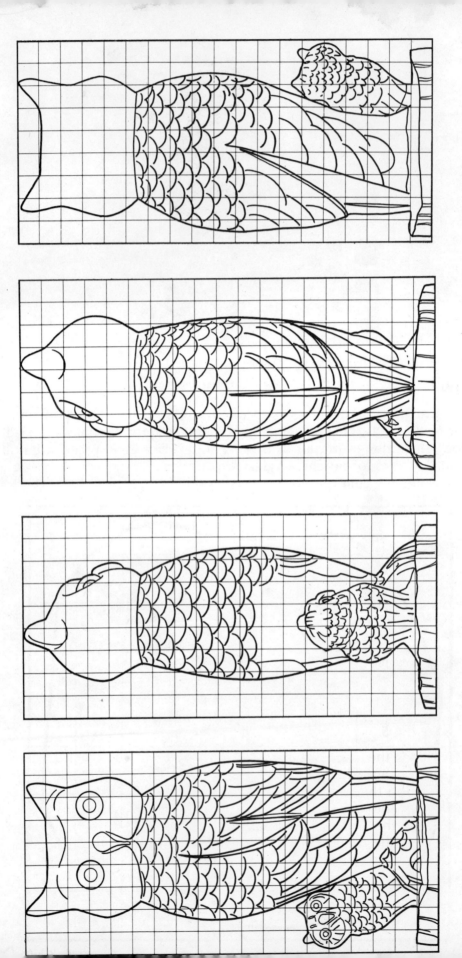

Using #134 cutter for rough carving and removing excess stock

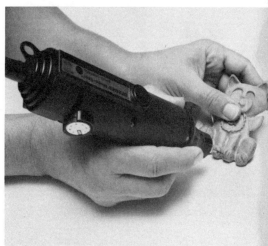

Fine detail carved with #105 engraving cutter

Using drum sander to rout edges

Gluing carving to bookend

BOOK ENDS

Here's the same cat that was used on the "Cookie-Cutter Christmas Tree" and that was enlarged to make the "Cat Memo Board" pictured on the first page of the color insert. Now it has been carved with the Moto-Tool to decorate a pair of bookends. The pattern was traced on the end of the board and most of the carving done before separating the carved piece from the board. This provided a "handle" so that the wood was easier to hold. The carved pieces were glued to

Inserting metal bookend

Designed and carved by Rosemarie Masotto

Finished project (right)

boards that had edges which had been routed and beveled with the drum sander, but other cutters or the Moto-Tool router could have been used. Cat's eyes were made from sequins, and whiskers are straight pins with the heads cut off after insertion.

TURTLE CLOCK

Here's a project to grace your coffee table; the turtle clock combines art with utility. The finished clock shown here was made from two pieces of basswood—1" for the bottom and ¾" for the top. It could also be made of harder wood such as walnut. The demonstration pieces are pine, but were used only so that the grain of the wood would be more visible. Pine is not recommended for this project.

Begin your project by tracing the pattern on wood, with the grain running from head to tail. Cut out the rough pattern on the Moto-Shop. The opening in the bottom should be cut to fit the clock you plan to use. They usually measure 2¼" in diameter, and can be

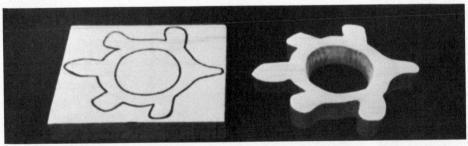

Pattern is transferred to wood and rough cut on jigsaw

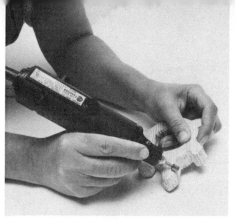
Base shaped and carved with Moto-Tool

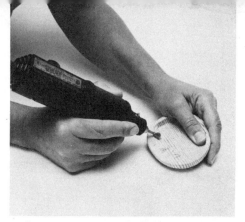
Hollowing out inner shell

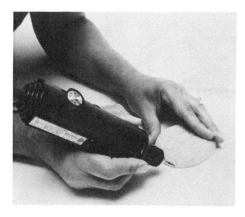

Insert clock or music box, or use turtle as jewel box

Small engraving cutter used for detail

obtained at clock shops and some craft and hobby stores. It is best to cut the opening slightly smaller and enlarge it carefully with the Moto-Tool drum sander until the clock mechanism slides in readily but tightly.

Use a #196 cutter to rough out the edges of both pieces, and roughly round off and hollow out the shell. Cut out the hollow with care so that the shell fits snugly over the top of the clock.

Shape the legs, head, and tail with #131 cutter. Smooth and round off the shell with the Moto-Tool drum sander using coarse grit. Cut in mouth, eyes, toes, and shell design with #106 engraving cutter. Turtle shells don't have a standard pattern; so you can vary this one to suit yourself.

Hand sand entire piece with fine abrasive paper until finish is smooth and ready for stain. If any fine details are lost in sanding, recut them with a #106 cutter.

Stain turtle, and finish with at least three coats of clear wood sealer, sanding lightly between coats. This piece was stained with Deft Spanish Walnut and sprayed with Deft Clear Wood Semi-gloss finish.

Finished clock

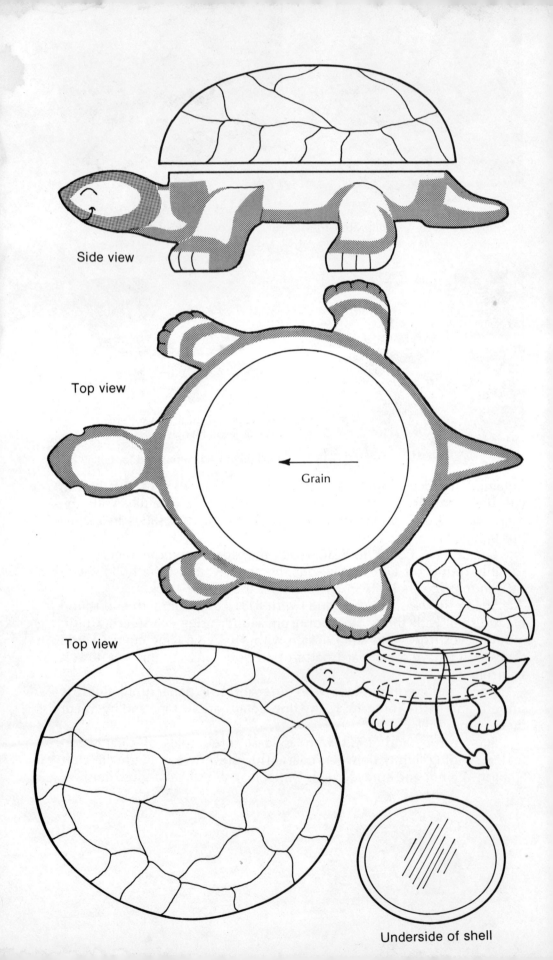

Side view

Top view

Grain

Top view

Underside of shell

Index